INSID

INSIDE FAITH
Praying for People in Prison

A revised and updated version of
Prayers for People in Prison

WILLIAM NOBLETT

DARTON · LONGMAN + TODD

First published in 2009 by
Darton, Longman and Todd Ltd
1 Spencer Court
140–142 Wandsworth High Street
London SW18 4JJ

ISBN 978–0–232–52733–9

A catalogue record for this book is available from the British Library.

*The opinions expressed in this book are those of the author and
contributors, and do not necessarily represent those of the
Prison Service Agency or the Ministry of Justice.*

Designed and produced by Sandie Boccacci
Set in 10/12pt Minion
Printed and bound in Great Britain by
Athenaeum Press, Gateshead, Tyne and Wear

Contents

This too I know – and wise it were
If each could know the same –
That every prison that men build
Is built with bricks of shame,
And bound with bars lest Christ should see
How men their brothers maim.

Oscar Wilde[1]

Foreword

If you've ever wondered what life was like inside a prison, step inside the pages and the prayers of this book. William Noblett, the Chaplain General of Prisons, opens the prison gates, unlocks the cell doors and takes you face to face with prisoners, many of whom have bared their souls to him. Here you will find testimonies and prayers that will leave you whispering to yourself, 'There but for the grace of God …'

There are many convictions that underpin these reflections and meditations. Imprisonment does not exclude or banish you from 'the cure of souls' which the Church has for each and every person in the country. There is nobody beyond the pale, no one out of reach of God's love. William helps us to see that, however marred the image of God may be in us, we can see the face of Christ in the eyes of every prisoner. Furthermore, whereas there will always be some who want to punish the offender forever by throwing away the key, people of faith believe that change is possible, even for the most persistent offender. But there is nothing naïve in these pages. The realities of evil and sin are recognised. The pain of the victim is fully acknowledged.

Along the way the Chaplain General gives a rare insight into the role of the Prison Chaplain, who occupies a unique position in the prison. The law requires the presence of Chaplains in prison to meet the spiritual needs of all offenders. People of faith believe that it is in the awakening of the spiritual awareness of offenders that they can acknowledge and repent of their offence, seek forgiveness and experience the remission of guilt and restoration.

This book is being published at an important time. There is increasing concern about the number of prisoners and about overcrowding in our prisons. It has sparked a national debate about crime and its causes, about who should be incarcerated and about how and why. Although not intended to be a contribution to this debate, this book offers a valuable voice which I, as Bishop to Prisons, believe should be heard. It speaks of the prisoner's humanity and appeals to our own; it offers a spiritual perspective and challenges our own spiritual attitudes.

In the famous story told by Jesus known as 'The Prodigal Son', there's an episode that is seldom commented upon. After the profligate younger brother has returned home, the father, who has waited patiently for his son's return, throws a party. On hearing about this, the dutiful elder son indignantly refuses to be drawn into the celebrations. His good father 'pleads' with him. The elder brother apparently cannot accept the repentance, reconciliation and restoration of his wayward younger brother.

Jesus tells this story to a group of hard-faced religious types who hate the sight of him associating with the 'low-life' of his day. This story serves as a poke in the eye to any society that writes off those at the bottom of the pile and refuses to accept either their humanity or their potential for restoration and rehabilitation. This goes to the heart of the debate about penal reform. Is prison a long-term warehouse for the incorrigible and the irredeemable or is it a greenhouse for the nurturing and the restoring of the flawed and the damaged?

It would be good to keep this question in mind as you go through the doors of these pages into the lives of the people who have opened their hearts to us here. Getting beneath their skin and going to where they are is precisely where God himself has gone. Ahead of us. In the person of Jesus he became a prisoner, endured a trial, was sentenced and punished. He knew what it's like to be a prisoner – despised and rejected. Presumably that's why Jesus told us that whenever we visited a prisoner – either in a cell or even through these pages – we would come face to face with him.

The Rt Revd James Jones,
Bishop of Liverpool & Anglican Bishop to Prisons

Foreword to the first edition

If my first few years as Archbishop are anything to go by, during my time I will write many forewords and reviews. I doubt, though, whether I will ever come across a book as brilliant and disturbing as this work by William Noblett. Brilliant, because the work presents a series of snapshots which, put together, catch prison life in its entirety. Disturbing, because as the jigsaw pieces fit together and present a whole picture, the reader begins a chilling descent into a world to which most of society would like to turn a blind eye.

The accounts are not lurid, with only the basic factual detail supplied. This ploy, of letting the reader's imagination unleash the full story, makes for interactive rather than passive reading, so that by the end of the book you do truly sit with those who minister in prison. What could be a very bleak work is redeemed on two counts. First, William Noblett is unashamed of his own humanity and frailty, and that honesty comes through as a shining beacon. Secondly, each brief account ends by moving naturally into prayer, very appropriate prayer, which draws magisterially from old and new.

This is a practical book, born out of a sensitive ministry in the prison service, one in which I was privileged to 'share the cure' during my time as Bishop of Wakefield, and now once more as Archbishop of York. It is a piece of writing I will often return to during my very different ministry, both for the accurate picture it gives of the prison world, and also for the insight it offers to the world which pretends to be far beyond prison walls. I am certain you will find it similarly invaluable, deepening your awareness of God 'in prison, his hideout in flesh and bone'.

+ David Ebor,
Archbishop of York

Acknowledgements

It is ten years since the publication of *Prayers for People in Prison*. This book is a revised and updated version. Much has happened during those ten years, and the prison service has changed and moved forward. It currently faces huge pressures of population management, with an equally significant new building programme.

Chaplaincy, too, has changed. It has become much more inclusive, reflecting a wide range of faiths, denominations and traditions. It has grown in numbers and in confidence as it seeks to serve the needs of prisoners, staff and faith communities.

What has not changed, however, is the essentials of ministry to and with prisoners and staff. This edition of the book incorporates many changes, but at its heart is a commitment to exploring something of that ministry to which chaplains, of all faiths, are called. What has changed for me, though, has been a step back from the experience of that ministry first-hand. As Chaplain General I am removed from the very ministry that inspired the first edition. But what I see and experience now, from a national perspective, is a hugely encouraging movement. Prison chaplains, of all faiths, are working side by side, committed to a vision of ministry that takes them into prison day by day, week by week, to be with and alongside some of the most marginalised members of our society. Some of the most dangerous, too, it has to be said. What chaplains do, in partnership with other staff and volunteers, is worthy of huge respect. I am proud of all that is done.

As Chaplain General, I have been fortunate to visit prisons and chaplaincies in a number of other countries, to learn something of their approach to ministry, and to share something of ours. Few, if any, are as inclusive in their approach, or as well resourced, as those in England and Wales.

The book is written from my own, Christian perspective,

but I have tried in this edition to provide some insight into the understanding of prison ministry of chaplains of other traditions.

All of the stories within this book are based on real situations, real people. Details, however, have been changed or obscured where necessary to protect the identity of any individual. Statistics, where they have been used, are from a wide range of sources. As always, they are capable of more than one interpretation, and are constantly changing. I have included websites where possible, but these, too, change!

I dedicate this book to all who live and work within our prisons and with whom I am privileged to share life and ministry.

I acknowledge with thanks, permission from the following to use and/or quote from their work:

Material from *Common Worship: Services and Prayers for the Church of England*, copyright © The Archbishops' Council, 2000. Extracts are reproduced by permission.
The Prison Reform Trust, for material from *Bromley Briefings*, various editions.
Revd Philip Berrigan.
Dietrich Bonhoeffer, brief extract from *Life Together*, © HarperCollins, San Francisco, 1975.
Churches Together in England and Wales, 'Called together', adapted from a prayer published in the *Week of Prayer for Christian Unity*, 1990.
The Prisons' Week Committee, 'Prisons' Week', used by permission.
Ben Butler, A4e, 'Education'.
Professor Andrew Coyle, 'Prisons, prisoners and imprisoners'.
John and Bernie Davis, 'Victims'.
Julia Flack, 'Living with risk'.
Cathy Hitchens, 'Vulnerability', 'A paradigm shift', 'Foreign nationals'.
Michael Hollings and Eta Gullick, from *It's Me, O Lord*. By permission of McCrimmon Publishing Co. Ltd.

Revd Canon Eric James, 'Why pray for people in prison?'

Revd T. M. Johns, 'Baptism', 'Welcome the stranger', 'A Prison Litany'.

Revd Dr L. M. McFerran, 'The Word across the prison world'.

Sister Elaine MacInnes OLM and The Phoenix Trust, 'Light behind bars'.

Revd Canon Keith Pound, 'Wholeness and the Therapeutic Community'.

Pierre Raphael, from 'The Chaplain's Prayer for Breath', from *Inside Riker's Island*, © 1990. Used by permission of Orbis Books.

Revd William Salmon, 'Confidentiality'.

R. S. Thomas, 'The Absence', 'The Prisoner'. Used with permission.

Professor David Wilson, 'Evil'.

Major David Emery SA, MBE and Kim Homer-Glister, 'Community Chaplaincy'.

Erwin James, 'Release'.

Brian Wren, extract from 'I come with joy' from *Piece Together Praise*, © 1971, 1995 Hope Publishing Company for the USA, Canada, Australia and New Zealand, and Stainer & Bell Ltd, London, for all other territories.

Oscar Wilde, *The Ballad of Reading Gaol*, Section 5, from *The Complete Oscar Wilde*, Michael O'Mara Books Ltd.

The Venerable Ajahn Khemadhammo OBE, Dr Shastry, Ahtsham Ali, Dr Indarjit Singh CBE, and Revd Michael Binstock, 'The spiritual roots of prison ministry'.

Revd Alan Ogier, 'Restorative Justice'.

Biblical quotations are from the New Revised Standard Version Bible: Anglicized Edition, © 1989, 1995, Division of Christian Education of the National Council of the Churches of Christ in the United States of America. Used by permission. All rights reserved.

Revd Brian Dodsworth, A brief history of prison chaplaincy in England and Wales.

Revd John Hargreaves, The word across the prison world.

Revd Fiona Eltringham, Young Offenders.

THE PENAL CONTEXT

Introduction

> The public conscience would be far more active if the
> punishment of imprisonment were abolished and we
> went back to the rack, the stake, the pillory, and the lash
> at the cart's tail ... It would be far better (for the offender)
> to suffer in the public eye; for among the crowd of sight-
> seers there might be a Victor Hugo or a Dickens, able and
> willing to make the sightseers think of what they are
> doing ... The prisoner has no such chance ... the secrecy
> of the prison makes it hard to convince the public that he
> is suffering at all.

George Bernard Shaw, with some exaggeration and in a different age, has nonetheless caught something of current views in
at least two respects. Firstly, the public mood and attitude
towards those who have committed crimes is very punitive,
and many would favour a return to the spectacle of corporal or
even capital punishment. Secondly, the continued rise in the
number of people being sent to prison (often in what seems to
be a case of 'first resort', rather than as a 'last resort') means that
almost 83,000 people are now imprisoned in England and
Wales, and with places for 96,000 planned by 2014. The cost to
the taxpayer is over £2 billion every year, without including the
capital cost of new prisons, or extensions to existing prisons.
Re-offending by ex-prisoners is estimated to cost society over
£11 billion each year.

Most prisoners will be released back into the community, at
some time, with about 30 people serving sentences for natural
life. The figures put England and Wales at the top of the
Western European league table for imprisonment, at 148
prisoners per 100,000 of population. (For comparisons see
'Prisons, prisoners, and imprisoners', page 54.)

Even now, at a time when there have been endless television programmes (fictional and factual) and newspaper and magazine articles about prisons, there is still a part of the prison world which is hidden from our view, and is secret. Part of the reason for this secrecy may be a fear that we will discover something of ourselves in those in prison. In the words of the newspaper columnist Polly Toynbee: 'Exploring the outer limits of human evil, we peer into our own dark souls and pleasurably frighten ourselves with our potential for sin.'

Part of this book is an attempt to bring the secrecy to light through the stories of individuals, and to bring to view something of the ministry of chaplains, and others, in a complex, emotional, and sometimes violent, environment. It also seeks to encourage ways in which representatives of faith communities might engage with those who have been released into the community.

R. S. Thomas, one of the finest poets of the twentieth century, and an Anglican priest, reminds us of the need to seek God in unexpected places, one of which is prison:

> We ransack the heavens,
> the distance between
> stars; the last place we look
> is in prison, his hideout
> in flesh and bone.
>
>   R. S. Thomas, 'The Prisoner'

This book has its primary location in 'the flesh and bone' of the lives of people in prison. Most of the pieces take the form of narratives, based in fact, but with some details changed to preserve the identity of individuals. Where possible the narratives reflect 'primary' and narrative theology; that is, theology which arises from the pastoral cycle of human experience and story, becomes reflective theology, and is then given expression in the language of prayer. As will be seen in the narratives, my concern is for the individual within the 'total institution'[2] which makes up the prison community. In a very limited way I have sought to make connections to other disciplines, notably psychology, and particularly as it provides insight into pastoral issues. Poetry and literature also help. I have sought to 'connect' the stories of individuals with the divine story, with God's story of relationship with us. Elie Wiesel, who suffered in the concentration camps of Auschwitz and Buchenwald during World War II, wrote that 'God made man because he loves stories.' In my writing, and in encouraging others to write, I have tried to provide stories which open a door into a space where we can search for something of the divine action in the lives of some difficult people, and in ourselves.

In a sermon to prison chaplains, the German theologian Karl Rahner explored how we might find Christ in prisoners, but also how we might find ourselves in them.[3] He wrote:

> We find ourselves in the prisoners when we see in them the hidden truth of our own situation. The truth that we are sinners; the truth that we are self-seekers; the truth that in a thousand different ways, crude or subtle, we are always trying to serve God and ourselves ... We may be free in a bourgeois, legal sense: we may be responsible for our actions, not only in the sight of men but also in the sight of God ... But if we have not been set free by the Spirit of God ... we are nevertheless helpless and hopeless prisoners in the prison of our guilt, our unsaved condition, our inability to perform any saving act.

He goes on to say:

> When you go from your own surroundings into a prison, you do not go out of a world of harmony, light and order into a world of guilt and unfreedom: you stay where you have been all the time. It is merely made clearer to your bodily sense what has been surrounding you all the time.

This book reflects the concerns of finding God and finding self within the community of God in prison. Few of us can do that alone, and I am pleased that a number of my colleagues, chaplains, other staff, and a number of prisoners, have felt able to contribute to narratives, or to submit their own. The stories contain the potential to transform us through prayer, and to change our understanding of God, and prisons. Kenneth Leech, Anglican priest and author, has put it like this: 'At heart prayer is a process of self-giving and of being set free from isolation. To pray is to enter into a relationship with God and to be transformed in him.'[4]

This book is not intended to provide some sort of theological legitimacy for a system which is working to its capacity, with increasing and constantly changing problems and priorities, and subject to efficiency savings (applied across Government departments.), and whose purpose and sense of direction can easily be lost in the responses forced upon it by the courts. Rather, this book seeks to provide, in part, a prophetic and ethical challenge to people of faith, through providing insight into the prison world, by applying theology and highlighting particular situations. At a time when the capacity of our prisons is expanding and with the public mood not one that reflects the need for a fundamental discussion on the purpose of imprisonment, or its alternatives, such a challenge seems apposite. Indeed, the Archbishop of Canterbury, Dr Rowan Williams, has called for a commission of enquiry into the penal system which, he says, is failing both offenders and victims because it can't cope with the primary need to change the behaviour of those convicted.[5]

This book reflects the way in which I seek the support of sympathetic and supportive individuals and groups in ministry with offenders in prison, and ex-offenders in the community. Through the book I hope to encourage Christians, and those of other faith traditions, to understand something of what is being done in their name, and to seek their prayerful, and practical, support.

The book is not intended primarily for prison chaplains, or for those who live or work within our prisons. Many of them will know more about prisons than I ever will, but I hope if they do read it, they may find it useful. It is intended as a resource book for concerned people of faith, who want to know more, and who may sit and pray with us who minister, in their name, in prison and in the community. The narratives and prayers may be used in private, or in public, though some will be too long for public use. The prayers are not prescriptive. People may feel free to use them in whatever way they wish, to adapt them, discard them, or incorporate them in some form into their own prayers. Some of the narratives may form an introduction to issues which could be used within a discussion group or Bible-study group.

In the 1564 Scottish Book of Common Order, the congregation is reminded of the need for offenders to be reconciled to God and to the Church, after repentance and the offering of satisfaction or reparation to the victim and the Church. The congregation is asked to embrace the offender as a brother, identifying with his situation. In addressing the penitent, the minister says, 'we all repute your fall to be our own; we accuse ourselves no less than we accuse you; now, finally, we join our prayers with yours, that we and you may obtain mercy.'

'We join our prayers with yours.' The identification, perhaps with reluctance and pain, of our humanity and fallenness with that of the offender, is deeply rooted in our Christian tradition, and here, given formal liturgical expression, it conveys a deep theological truth about our need to hold each other in prayer. It also reminds us that all but about 30 of those 83,000 prisoners will return to the community at some point. As a community we need to think about how we will receive them. For us as faith communities, the question is imperative.

As far as I am aware, there is no comparable book available to people anywhere. It is the result of the generosity of all those who have contributed, and of all those who live and work within our prisons. Despite signs to the contrary, God is here, present and active in the lives of many people. Most of the time, however, he has to be sought out. Through this book we can do that together, and perhaps in so doing, be transformed.

Information

In order to view current population figures, visit the Prison Service website:

www.hmprisonservice.org.uk

or

www.justice.gov.uk/publications/populationincustody.htm

For an update on penal policy, visit:

www.justice.gov.uk/publications/prison-policy-update.htm

Why pray for people in prison?

John had been a popular civil servant, a good boss in his place of work. He had been conscientious, worked hard, enjoyed his own company, and his home environment. He was articulate, interested in music, especially classical. He read widely and had a good knowledge of English literature. Always ready to discuss his current reading, he was an avid follower of world events. Over many weeks we sat together and talked at length.

Eric too, had worked hard over a number of years. Single and lonely, he had persevered with his education programme despite failing health. Finally, he obtained the Bachelor of Science degree in Sociology and Psychology which he so wanted. He constantly gave me papers to read. Abstruse and academic, devoid of 'plain English', I found them demanding. In hospital, he asked me to pray with him as he prepared for his death.

On the face of it, both men had much in common with many others in the population. Eric's request for prayer would seem reasonable under the circumstances. His victims, however, were just a few years older than my young son. Boys whose lives had been 'snuffed'[6] out by a man whose quest for sexual gratification was uncontrolled.

John was a serial killer. His killings had been in double figures. Reviled by the media, he was greatly feared within the prison. His crimes offended me deeply.

When Eric asked for my prayers, and when I sat in a cell in the Segregation Unit with John, I had to draw deeply on the well of my compassion, my understanding of prayer, and of God. Why pray for, and with, these men? Surely such people are beyond redemption, cannot be offered salvation, do not deserve our compassion? Such questions are frequently directed to me, and I regularly ask them of myself. In my heart

I feel I know the answer, but my intellect is hard pressed to give a justification, even to myself.

With both men I was often reduced to silence, unable and unwilling to articulate the depth of my revulsion for their crimes. Whilst I could separate the 'sin from the sinner' in my mind, my heart was telling me something very different. Sometimes I wanted to respond by shouting out my incredulity, my lack of understanding, and my pain for those who had died. In private, my thoughts and prayers became a silence and a shouting, as they frequently do.

In the book, *It's Me, O Lord*, by Michael Hollings and Eta Gullick,[7] there is a description of prayer which I have found useful in helping me to pray:

> The important thing about prayer is that it is almost indefinable. You see, it is: hard and sharp, soft and loving, deep and inexpressible, shallow and repetitious, a groaning and a sighing.
>
> A silence and a shouting, a burst of praise digging deep down into loneliness, into me. Loving. Abandonment to despair, a soaring to heights which can be only ecstasy, dull plodding in the greyness of mediocre being – laziness, boredom, resentment.
>
> Questing and questioning, calm reflection, meditation, cogitation. A surprise at sudden joy, a shaft of light, a laser beam. Irritation at not understanding, impatience, pain of mind and body hardly uttered or deeply anguished.
>
> Being together, the stirring of love shallow, then deeper, then deepest. A breathless involvement, a meeting, a longing, a loving, an inpouring, a drowning, a swooning, more.

I think prayer is almost indefinable and the more I seek to pray, particularly prayers of intercession, the more difficult I find it to articulate what it is I am doing. And the more I find it hard to do so, the more I am thrown back on the love of God. I know

God's love for me as an individual, with all my failings, and through the knowledge of his love for me I know of his love for others, without exception. It is not possible for me to say that God loves some and not others, that he loves the righteous and not the sinner. 'I have come to call not the righteous but sinners' (Mark 2:17b). It is the certainty of the unconditional love and the unmerited grace of God which enables me daily to enter into the lives of those who are considered by many in society to be 'beasts and perverts, monsters, maniacs, serial killers, thugs, brutes, hooligans, junkies, parasites', and worse.

'We love because he first loved us' (1 John 4:19). In the example of Jesus, the Christ, in his compassion for those on the margins of society, cast out by society, made the scapegoats, there lies a call to us to take the pain, the hurt, the oppression, the brokenness and the brutalisation of prison seriously and to say it cannot be accepted as the norm, that it is abnormal and unacceptable for us, who are made in the image of God.

It is this, perhaps, to which Oscar Wilde alludes in his *Ballad of Reading Gaol*, quoted at the beginning of this book. Wilde also wrote: 'The prison system – a system so terrible that it hardens their hearts whose hearts it does not break, and brutalises those who have to carry it out no less than those who have to submit to it.'[8] This echoes the words of a former Conservative Government Minister who said that 'prison succeeds only in making bad people worse.'

It is not the totality of the prison experience, however, and the vision held before staff, as verbalised in the Statement of Purpose, is: Her Majesty's Prison Service serves the public by keeping in custody those committed by the courts. Our duty is to look after them with humanity and help them lead law-abiding and useful lives in custody and after release.' Prisons are also places of hope and compassion, where staff seek to combine the need for humane custodial care, and rehabilitation. Prison officers, in particular, seek to hold the tension between these demands, and our prayers are needed to undergird their work.

I have to acknowledge my part in the brutalisation, as one

whose representative presence as a Christian priest lends some form of legitimacy to the prison system and all it stands for. And because it has had a profound influence on my personal life, and that of my family. Prison has led me to be much more suspicious of people, to be more critical, less tolerant, more short-tempered. This is a reflection of the social and environmental influence of prison. It exacts a high price on all who live and work behind its walls.

Ironically, it is because of my ministry in such a place – with all its effects, personal and professional, and the painful questions which it asks of me, my faith, and my understanding of God – that I discover and acknowledge my dependence on God. Philip Berrigan, an American priest imprisoned for his opposition to his country's involvement in armed conflict, wrote about what had helped him to remain free in prison:

> I have discovered two things about prayer since entering prison: first that when I pray humbly and honestly I can hack this life even at its bitterest. When I don't pray, I cannot. When I don't pray I begin to apply to life the only power I really know – violence. Inch by inch I begin to disintegrate, and so do my relationships with others. I begin to brood about the injustice of this experience, and the dark side of my soul assumes control. But when I pray I accept my dependency on God and on my friends. And a love not my own is lent me. And I can continue.

Philip Berrigan wrote as a prisoner, but I fully concur with his words and his experience. Why do I stay in prison ministry? Because it is here that I need God more than anywhere else. Alexander Solzhenitsyn, reflecting on his time of incarceration in Russian Gulags, said, 'Bless you prison ... for it was there that I discovered that the meaning of earthly existence lies in the development of the soul.'

The unmerited grace of God, so much a part of the Gospel proclaimed by St Paul, is rooted in the concept of the unconditional love of God. The word 'grace' comes from the same root as 'gracious' and 'graciousness', virtues which one might think are often lacking in prison. And yet, I can say with confidence, 'But God proves his love for us in that while we were sinners Christ died for us' (Rom. 5:8). In that act of love, I can identify and accept a gift, freely offered, which I have done nothing at all to deserve or earn. In my gratitude I turn to prayer, and in my ministry I strive to reflect something of that unconditional love and unmerited grace in an environment which is often contemptuous of the notion of love, and of God.

I frequently use one of the prayers suggested at the conclusion of the Alternative Order of Confirmation included in the Prayer Book as proposed in 1928. In its more modern translation it reads:

> Go forth into the world in peace;
> be of good courage;
> hold fast that which is good;
> render to no one evil for evil;
> strengthen the fainthearted; support the weak;
> help the afflicted; honour everyone;
> love and serve the Lord,
> rejoicing in the power of the Holy Spirit.
>
> Based on 1 Thessalonians 5:13–22

In starting this chapter I deliberately portrayed some of the positive aspects of John and Eric's lives. I was being selective about their good points, as I could so easily identify the bad points. I do not want to ignore the bad, or to emphasise only the good. It does not mean ignoring their crimes, the sins which they have committed, but it does mean continuing to show them 'respect, esteem, reverence, or worth', as the *Oxford English Dictionary* defines 'honour'. The Christian belief in God the creator means that nothing we do can entirely mar his image in us. No matter how hard I have found it to do so, I have always sought 'to find that of God in everybody', as the Quakers say. The Christian writer, Virgil Georghiu, in a piece much quoted by prison chaplains, has written:

> The police seek in every human being a murderer;
> the wise man and the philosopher seek in every
>   murderer a human being.
> We Christians seek God in every person ... even in
>   murderers.
> And each of us will find what he seeks:
> the police will find their murderer;
> the philosophers will find their human beings;
> and we, we shall find God in every person.[9]

I believe that in 'seeking God in every person', honour can be accorded in a similar way to the way in which Jesus honoured those whom he met. In his dealing with the woman taken in adultery (John 8:1–11), he is gracious towards her, according her respect as a human being. In a sense he 'honours' her, at a time when many would have been calling for a harsh sentence.

When he tells the remarkable story of the Prodigal Son, or, more properly, the Loving Father, Jesus makes it clear that the father gives honour to the returning son as a gift, despite all that has gone before. He nowhere suggests there are some actions, some situations from which it would be impossible for the son to come home. Nor is there any suggestion of rejection by the father because of anything which the son may have done. It is a dramatic story, based on principles of Restorative Justice (see p. 230) about repentance, forgiveness and restoration, themes that are central in Luke and Acts. The son acknowledges his wrongdoing and says he is not worthy, and in so doing he receives a deep and undeserved kindness, the unmerited grace of the father. The honour and dignity we accord to each other is a mark of our understanding of the honour and dignity God freely gives to us. For me, this idea is summed up in one of the prayers for use after communion in *Common Worship*:

> Father of all,
> we give you thanks and praise,
> that when we were still far off

you met us in your Son and brought us home.
Dying and living, he declared your love,
gave us grace, and opened the gate of glory.
May we who share Christ's body live his risen life;
we who drink his cup bring life to others;
we whom the Spirit lights give light to the world.
Keep us firm in the hope you have set before us,
so we and all your children shall be free,
and the whole earth live to praise your name;
through Christ our Lord.

The declaration of love, the giving of grace, the wonderful symbolism of God in Christ meeting us and bringing us, the undeserving and sinful, home, is powerful. In all of these instances the compassion of Christ and the experience of salvation are intimately linked, even where the person who is offered salvation is unable to make restitution for his offences.

One of the criminals crucified with Jesus (Luke 23:33f) receives the promise of paradise in the hour of his death, without any opportunity to lead a new life, or to make restitution. Only Luke records the words of that repentant criminal and the response of Jesus: 'today you will be with me in Paradise' (Luke 23:43). Whilst the words 'forgiveness' and 'salvation' are not used, they are implied in Jesus' words. And as Jesus is crucified, we hear him pray for the forgiveness of those who are crucifying him: 'Father, forgive them; for they do not know what they are doing.'

In the parable of the tax-collector and the Pharisee (Luke 18:9–14), contrary to what Jesus' listeners would have anticipated, God answers the prayers of the tax-collector and not those of the Pharisee. As far as we know, this minor tax-collector was not involved in reparation and those who heard Jesus must have been overwhelmed by the implications of this sort of story. Later, we see salvation for the chief tax-collector, Zacchaeus (Luke 19:1–10), as Jesus takes the initiative and invites himself to his house, and into his transformed life.

In the parable of the Good Samaritan (Luke 10:25–37), the

most unlikely of people performs an extraordinary act of compassion. Such stories were, and are, radical and alternative teaching, and they are at the very heart of Christian understanding. It is clearly seen in the way Jesus is portrayed as someone who brings the outcast, the stranger, the enemy, the betrayer, home and gives each one a place at the banquet of God's reign.

In one of his collections of sermons, *Judge Not*, Canon Eric James[10] speaks on the text, 'Honour everyone. Love the family of believers. Fear God. Honour the Emperor' (1 Pet. 2:17). He says:

> To me, perhaps the most moving scene in the whole New Testament is when Judas comes with a crowd, with swords and staves, and betrays Jesus to them with a kiss. What does Jesus say to his betrayer? Does he *dis*honour him? Does he refrain from honouring him? He says to him: 'Friend, wherefore art thou come?' The commentary on that verse in the beautiful 14th Century book of mystical German writings *Theologica Germanica*, is: 'He said to Judas when he betrayed him: "Friend, wherefore art thou come?" Just as if he had said: "Thou hatest me, and art mine enemy, yet I love thee and am thy friend." As though God in human nature was saying: "I am pure, simple Goodness, and therefore I cannot will or desire or rejoice in, or do anything but goodness. If I am to reward thee for thy evil and wickedness, I must do it with goodness, for I am and have nothing else."' That is to me the very basis of honouring not just good people, whoever they may be, but *everyone*.

Canon James, as Preacher to Gray's Inn for many years, was regularly preaching to those involved with the law – judges, barristers, solicitors, law students – and his exposition of what it means to 'honour everyone' has had a considerable influence on my thinking over many years. It is so closely related to the emphasis in our prisons to treat people with dignity. As

Christians we are called to the counter-cultural practice of loving our enemies, of praying for those who offend against us, of showing compassion to those in need, of honouring everyone, difficult though it may sometimes be.

Such ideas and practices are often contrary to the way in which society thinks, where hatred and retribution are regularly seen as normal, and even healthy, and where they are occasionally accorded divine sanction. The way of Christ, it seems to me, is the opposite to such a view and it is reflected in prayer for those who most hurt us, in prayer for those in prison, and those imprisoned by their passions, hurts and distorted images of self and others.

'We never feel so good as when we are punishing someone,' said Bertrand Russell. The element of truth in this thought must be acknowledged, but it needs to be challenged by Christian people whose Lord offered a radically different alternative in the example of his love and compassion. In a society which seems increasingly punitive, Christians are called to offer a different approach to the person in prison. I acknowledge the difficulties in any such approach and I don't always find it easy when faced with some of the people I meet, but as Eric James has said: 'We dare not admit defeat in the task of reclaiming and restoring this person and that from whatever evil he or she has fallen into, for our religion teaches us that Christ himself lived and died to reclaim not some sorts of sinners but all sorts.'

A brief history of prison chaplaincy in England and Wales

> Lord, what would become of the prisoner if Christian society, that is, the Church, were to reject him as civil society rejects him? ... there could not be a greater despair than that for the prisoner.

Fyodor Dostoevsky, the great Russian novelist, and a Christian, had been a prisoner. He knew the depths of human failing, and developed an extraordinary insight into the mind and character of prisoners. He lived amongst those who had committed incredible violence and acts of depravity. Of his time in prison at Omsk, he wrote:

> I consider those four years as a time during which I was buried alive and shut up in a coffin. Just how horrible that time was I have not the strength to tell you ... it was indescribable, unending agony, because each hour, each minute weighed upon my soul like a stone ...

The conditions were appalling, and yet, he says:

> even in penal servitude, among thieves and bandits, in the course of four years I finally succeeded in discovering human beings. Can you believe it; among them are deep, strong, magnificent characters, and how cheering it was to find gold under the coarse surface ...

More recently, echoing the first quote from Dostoyevsky, a prisoner in a high-security jail in England wrote:

Tell my mother that every prison has a chaplain, and no matter what others say about us, no matter who may abandon us, the Church never will, and neither will our Lord. He knew what it was like to be deserted in the Garden.

In the Licence given by each Anglican Bishop to those priests who minister within his Diocese (including prison chaplains), are the words, 'Receive the cure of souls, which is both mine and yours.'

For me, these are powerful words, bestowing on both parties a responsibility for shared ministry in the prison context. The Bishop represents the wider Church of which we are but one part. We who minister in prison have a responsibility to the Church. This is also true for chaplains of all faiths and denominations as they represent their respective traditions. Part of what this book seeks to do is to fulfil that responsibility through providing an insight into prison life and into the ministry which it demands.

The Church's presence in English and Welsh prisons has been officially recognised since 1773 when an Act of Parliament authorised Justices of the Peace to appoint salaried chaplains to their local prisons. The salary was not to exceed £50 per annum, and was to come from the county rates.

It may be a surprise to some, but up until this time, most jails were privately run, including one or two under the control of bishops! The profit motive meant that prisoners were charged fees for the services provided for them whilst in prison. In the Fleet Prison, made famous by Charles Dickens, charges were on a sliding scale, with an Archbishop expected to pay an entrance fee of £10! At that time, few were willing to pay for the services of a clergyman, and formal acts of worship took place infrequently. With the introduction of salaried chaplains, the situation slowly changed. Interestingly, the opening of the Wolds Prison in April 1992 brought to an end a period of over 100 years in which all prisons in the United Kingdom had been directly managed by central government.

Private-sector involvement in the penal system had returned.

In the nineteenth century, clergy were at first appointed on a part-time basis and they had a purely pastoral role. In recent times a former Archbishop of Canterbury reiterated this role:

> In talking to prison Chaplains I have emphasised their pastoral role. This is in line with the commission given to bishops, priests and deacons of the Church of England at their ordination, when the pastoral emphasis is over-whelming; they are to provide for the flock and to minister to the sheep who have gone astray.

The first chaplains attended to the sick and those about to be executed, but some found their task depressing and unrewarding. Complaints arose that such men (*sic*) could not do much in a prison which echoed with profanity and blasphemy. The same might be thought true today! But ministry is partly about faithfulness and perseverance, and the continuous and renewed call to be where God's people are, in whatever circumstances.

The office and role of chaplain was given much greater significance following the powerful influence and advocacy of John Howard, whose famous book, *The State of the Prisons in England and Wales,* appeared in 1777. Howard had visited prisons in Holland where services were regularly held in the prison chapel. Howard urged that similar arrangements should be made in English prisons, and he made a plea to jailers not to hinder prisoners from attending 'divine worship'. Robert Peel's Gaol Act of 1823 gave more careful definition of the responsibilities of the chaplain, and made it possible for the stipend to be as much as £250 per annum.

Between 1816 and 1877, central government had responsibility only for convict prisoners, and when the first of these prisons, Millbank, opened in 1816, the Church's mission with prisoners was given much greater stimulus. In Millbank, which was designed to hold 1000 prisoners, the atmosphere was very different from that which had prevailed in the much smaller, county jails. The experiment was firmly built on the conviction that evangelism was the answer to crime. The chapel stood at the very heart of the penitentiary, literally as well as metaphorically, and this was to provide chaplains with a unique opportunity. The authorities directed that every prisoner must attend religious services and must behave reverently in chapel. Going one step further in one prison, they even made the chaplain the governor of the establishment. He was able to order the programme to suit his avowed aim, and all the rules were geared to achieve the object of religious exercises, by which the convicts would be reformed. Each warder (called Prison Officers since 1921) carried a Bible, and was expected to quote Scripture at appropriate moments.

The experiment was not considered a success, however, and it proved that even the coercion of the penitentiary cannot bring about change without a heart that is open to the love of God.

Other prisons were soon to follow at Parkhurst, Portland and Dartmoor. In 1842, Pentonville Prison was opened. Known as the Model Prison, it was the first of 54 prison buildings constructed to a similar design during the next six years, and of which, most are still in use today. As we have seen so often, the model was taken from the American experience, and transported to England. Essentially a system of solitary confinement for all prisoners, it relied on discipline carried to extreme lengths. It came from Pennsylvania, where faith in the value of solitude as a means of reforming criminals was almost fanatical. Prisoners were placed in cells, and could be shut off from human companionship for many years – a situation still experienced by prisoners in oppressive regimes in some countries, even today. The prisoners stayed in their cells for divine worship, many desperately trying to catch sound of a human voice, with the preacher standing in the corridor. In American maximum-security ('super-max') prisons, worship (and many other activities) is conducted by television linkage to each cell.

At the time, the deprivation of human fellowship was designed to encourage communion with God. Reminiscent of

monks in their cells, it has been suggested that the concept of
prison as we know it came from a monograph written by a
seventeenth-century Benedictine monk in which he recom-
mends that wrongdoers be reformed by sampling a spell of
monastic life. In the 'model prison' the chaplain's role was a
major one. To men desperate for companionship, he was to
dispense the consolation of the Gospel.

The task proved to be impossible. Even with an assistant, it
was not easy to get around all the cells, and eventually a compromise was agreed. The prisoners would be taken to Chapel
on Sundays for worship, but in order to maintain their isolation, they were made to wear hoods over their heads, and to sit
in individual boxes during the service, so they could see the
preacher, but not each other. (A fine example of this design
may be seen in Lincoln Castle.)

Eventually, this system of solitary confinement, which had
partly come about as a protest against the indiscriminate herd-
ing of all kinds of prisoners in enforced cohabitation, gave way
to one of classification and training, much as we know it today.

The chaplain's role, however, continued to be enshrined in
the various Prison Acts, up to and including that of 1952, the
most recent. In a sense, the pastoral role has become part of
the requirement placed on chaplains through what are called
'Statutory Duties', contained both within the Act, and in various Prison Rules. Effectively, they are what most chaplains
would see as being important pastorally, as they involve seeing
prisoners as they come into the prison (Receptions), and daily
if they are in the Segregation Unit, the Health Centre, or the
Vulnerable Prisoner Unit. Additionally, people are seen in their
cells, at worship, their workplace, or in groups. No member of
the chaplaincy team is limited by that which is defined as
'statutory', and these duties are but the springboard to involvement with the whole life of the prison, in different ways, and at
different levels, with prisoners and staff, and their families.

In recent years, and with the increased emphasis on the 'end
to end' management of offenders, from pre- to post-custody,
there has been a significant development in the concept of

'chaplaincy'. Building on work done in Canada, a number of community chaplaincy schemes have developed in this country, providing ongoing care to a small number of those released into the community. Community chaplaincies offer practical and spiritual support to ex-offenders, helping them to restore their lives, and to re-integrate into wider society.

Prison chaplains, and community chaplains too, have been described as 'standing at the cross-roads of human experience, able to meet with men and women, often in crisis.' Sense needs to be made of their waiting, their pain and, perhaps, their guilt. Prison represents an extreme human experience, and it is here that people sometimes encounter God, with joy and hope, and occasionally, with a sense of sins forgiven.

The ministry to those in prison will always take various forms, but the purpose must be to proclaim something of the unconditional love of God. It is not about being in a position to moralise, to impose a particular viewpoint. It is about encouraging a process of growth and self-discovery, which may take much time. For many chaplains, they can only 'plant the seed', and hope and pray that it will be nurtured.

Chaplains, as with all members of prison staff, have to face change in structures, organisation and the pastoral circumstances of prisoners. For some Muslim chaplains in particular, the rise in the number of prisoners sentenced (or on remand) for extremist-related issues raises new questions, new opportunities and new fears. Such issues are incredibly complex, and whilst some Christian chaplains faced similar issues with Irish Republican Army (IRA) prisoners some years ago, Al Qaeda-inspired extremism is on a different level, and of a different magnitude. We have to hold to the conviction that, however desolating an experience it may be, prison can be a stimulus to provoke real choices, and transformation of lives. At the heart of each person who ministers in prison, there is a faith rooted in the reality and purpose of God, in whom all things are possible.

Chaplains of the Christian tradition are called by God, and by their Church, to a shared ministry in a difficult place. Their task is the joyful proclamation of the love of God, and they are in prison to be used, to be accessible and available to give simple, and, sometimes, costly care. At other times they are there to indulge in what may appear to some as 'useless presence'. A former Roman Catholic colleague came into my office just days before Christmas. He was just managing to hold back his tears. 'Look at this,' he said. It was a Christmas card, given to him by a prisoner, one of his congregation, and signed with his prison number. When my colleague went to see the man, a lifer, to ask him why he had signed it in this way, he replied, truthfully, 'I don't see myself as a person any more, just as a number.'

Another chaplain writes: 'Unless imprisonment can become part of a journey toward a goal rather than a desert of purposeless waiting, the chaplain's help is of limited value. Endless patience is required to stay present with people who cannot yet choose a road – for, in the end, it can never be chosen for them.'

In the book of Ezekiel, the people of God are in exile in Babylon. Ezekiel's account of his pastoral ministry includes the words, 'I came to them in captivity, and I sat where they sat ...' (Ezek. 3:15). In this book, you are invited to sit with those of us who minister in prison, to share our ministry, but above all, to pray with us.

Information

Chaplaincy HQ is located within the Directorate of Commissioning and Operational Policy at NOMS Headquarters. The National Offender Management Service (NOMS) was created in 2004. NOMS is the system through which correctional services and interventions are commissioned and provided to protect the public and reduce re-offending.

NOMS bridges the divide between custody and community, helping to deliver punishments and reparation and co-ordinate rehabilitative, health, educational, employment and housing opportunities for offenders to reduce re-offending.

A new structure was introduced to NOMS in April 2008 as

part of the reorganisation of the Ministry of Justice. NOMS and the Headquarters and regional structures of HM Prison Service were streamlined into a single organisation responsible for front-line delivery and running of HM Prison Service, overseeing the contracts of privately run prisons, managing probation performance and creating probation trusts.

As from April 2009 each of the nine regions in England and Wales saw the appointment of a Director of Offender Management (DOM) who is accountable for all probation and prison delivery, working with individual persons (public and private) and through probation boards or Trusts. DOMs are responsible for performance to the NOMs Board through the Chief Operating Officer.

A paradigm shift

The late David Bosch, a South African theologian, in his magisterial work, Transforming Mission, wrote: 'a paradigm shift always means both continuity and change, both faithfulness to the past and boldness to engage the future, both constancy and contingency, both tradition and transformation ... to be both evolutionary and revolutionary.' He said that the transition 'from one paradigm to another is not abrupt', and the agenda is 'always one of reform, not replacement', with 'creative tension between the new and the old'.

The changes in chaplaincy have been many, with the creation of an inclusive, multi-faith approach that respects the integrity of each tradition, but celebrates difference as much as that which is common to the faiths; a chaplaincy that believes in serving the common good of staff and prisoners.

It would be impossible to catalogue the changes that have taken place in the space available, difficult to capture something of 'the new' which draws on the commitment and understanding of chaplains of all faith traditions.

One chaplain who 'caught the vision' and gave a talk at the dedication of the new chaplaincy area in her prison, captures something of where chaplaincy is, now. She also says something about how we understand shared space in places where space is limited:

Since 2001, there has been a paradigm shift in Prison Chaplaincy.

We have pioneered Multi-Faith Teams and have left colleagues in the Forces, hospitals and other sector ministries way behind. Our prison chaplaincies don't give lip service to the Multi-Faith ideal. We have created the *reality* and continue to build on the vision of inclusiveness set out by the Chaplain

General. A vision that seemed impossible to achieve but one that, nevertheless, we see in all its glory here today.

This Dedication has been a long time coming. It is over four years since we were told we were going into a new building and circumstances have meant having to cancel two previously arranged services and, you know what? I am very grateful it has actually taken so long.

The service we share in today is unlike anything we expected. It is a unique expression of a Chaplaincy and its Team and how they have learnt to find the common ground, holy ground – together. There is real parity amongst us. We each have our part to play and no one role is more important than another.

The new building is our *shared* sacred space. Its feel-good factor comes from the prayers of all its worshippers. In this space alone, the atmosphere is created by Christian and Muslim alike. Together we create holy ground even though we worship here at different times of the week.

It has become glaringly obvious that no one Faith has the monopoly on holiness. All play their part in filling the vacuum with their prayers, meditation and praise. We have used the imagery of a rainbow to express visually our vision of our Chaplaincy here. Notice how each colour is vibrant, distinctive and special. The colours can stand alone and they have their own depth and richness, but together and only together, they form a stunning arc of contrasts, a bow that depends on each brilliant hue connecting with the others and so becoming interdependent. There's no mixing the colours. This is multi-faith, not inter-faith. It isn't like the child who takes the colours in his paint-box and stirs them all up together into one disgustingly, yucky mess. No. This is about mutual respect. It is about accepting our differences and not feeling threatened by them. It is about honouring and valuing every human being, whatever their faith or creed, and following the maxim of doing unto others what we would like done to ourselves.

As Chaplains we have the duty and responsibility to not only accept the faith of others, but to ensure that we enable all to worship freely, safely and with dignity.

I think I can speak on behalf of all my colleagues when I say we are enriched by this whole challenging experience and I, for one, wouldn't have missed it for the world, not for the world – which leads me onto our place in this unique community, this international prison, this microcosm of the United Nations. There are nearly 70 nationalities within these walls. We represent the world at large and I believe, deeply, that we have a unique opportunity to make a difference, a real difference for good.

As Chaplains, we recognise that we influence lives. We help folk in the good times and the bad. We challenge and encourage, and our shared ministry is prophetic. That ministry lies at the very heart of this prison's life and the lives of all who live, work or visit here. Whatever we bring – our faith offerings – our hopes and dreams – our prayers – and, yes, our influence – all these things will leave this place to travel far and wide. Our influence is therefore global. The experience this prison creates within its walls will travel around the world. What a responsibility that is. What an opportunity. How important it is for us to go on developing a culture of tolerance, harmony and peace.

These are truly exciting times. There is a real 'wow' factor involved here. This long-awaited day has come at just the right moment. We have told our stories, read our scriptures, said our prayers, sung songs. We have dedicated ourselves and this place. We have, together, made a rainbow and laid on it symbols of our Faiths, our treasure. I hope we will all leave this service encouraged, inspired and knowing that we not only can make a difference but that we inevitably do and that we are morally bound to ensure that it is for good, not ill. The world outside cries out to be healed. Its peoples are torn apart by their differences, and by violence. The finest offering we can bring is that of compassion, tolerance and unconditional love, and where more appropriate a place to begin than here in this city, an ancient centre of pilgrimage, a city that welcomes the stranger unreservedly. Who better than those of us here in this truly multi-faith, multi-cultural, international community?

I do believe that a single person can change the world. It has happened, has it not?

What difference, then, can we make together? Let us acknowledge our differences, respect them, be unafraid of them. Let us glory in our individual contributions without apology. Let us enjoy being who we are whilst appreciating the specialness of our neighbours. We have dedicated this Chaplaincy and its Chaplains, but the greatest dedication of all would be if, like the rainbow, we strive together to bring hope to the four corners of the world just because we can, just because we really can.

> Therefore it was called Babel, because there the Lord confused the language of all the earth; and from there the Lord scattered them abroad over the face of all the earth.
> Genesis 11:9

Peace to Chaplaincy,
peace to those who love it and who leave their love
*   in it.*
Peace to those who bring themselves,
their prayers,
their worship.
Peace to those who bring their silence,
their presence.
Peace to those who come seeking hope,
calm, forgiveness.
Peace to those who bring their broken dreams,
their pain,
their desolation.
Peace to those who bring respect,
for all who come,
for themselves.
Peace to those who come with a vision.
Peace to those who offer holiness.

Peace – Peace – Peace.

The spiritual roots of prison ministry

In 'A paradigm shift', recent changes in chaplaincy have been well laid out. The move to a more inclusive approach has been exciting and rewarding. In this section, Prison Service Faith Advisers from the Buddhist, Hindu, Jewish, Muslim and Sikh traditions write about their understanding of the spiritual roots of prison ministry. The spiritual roots of a Christian understanding of prison ministry are expressed in earlier sections of this book.

Buddhism

Angulimala, the Buddhist Prison Chaplaincy, is named after a notorious serial killer who had been responsible for almost a thousand murders when he met the Buddha. That encounter ended with him throwing away his weapons, renouncing violence and meekly following the Buddha back to the monastery, where he took up the life of a Buddhist monk. He eventually achieved Enlightenment and became one of the *Arahants* (Enlightened Disciples).

There are important lessons to be drawn from this story. First, we must never forget that people can and will and do change, and that we have a duty to offer what help and guidance we can for people to change for the better. Next, although the Buddhist texts give little detail about what passed between the Buddha and Angulimala, it seems clear that it was the Buddha's example – his serenity, fearlessness, love and compassion – that stopped Angulimala in his tracks. And then lastly, Angulimala wasn't condemned to be punished and hurt or written off as no good, either by the Buddha or by the King when, out searching for Angulimala to arrest and execute him, he discovered him living as a monk with the Buddha. This, then, is what I hope for – that instead of condemning people who have done wrong, viewing them as outcasts and wanting to hurt them, I hope we can learn to give prisoners our love and friendship and the chance to change for the better and even, by abandoning all greed, hatred and delusion, to perfect themselves.

Hinduism

Karma is the doctrine for explaining the causes of suffering on the part of one's self, and for explaining the pleasure others might be enjoying. Hence it is not right to condemn anybody who is under a sentence. Instead, appropriate sympathy and care have to be extended by others for those who are serving their sentences. The sentence purifies the guilty from their sins. A ruler, or state, has the duty to sentence the guilty for these reasons – to purify himself, and society. Nobody would be punished twice for an offence.

> *Sukhasya duhkhasya na kopi data, aham karomeeti vrtha-abhimanah. Anyah karoteeti kubuddhiresha, sva-Karma-sutra-grathito hi lokah.*

Translation from the Sanskrit:

> Our happiness and unhappiness are not given by out-siders; they are our reflections. If we think we are the doers and we created our happiness, those thoughts are the products of our ego. If we blame somebody else to have caused our unhappiness, that wickedness of finding fault should immediately be rectified. This is fact: The entire world is structured with various threads of Karma which are natural to the creation.

In fact, the sentence is for all: the person sentenced undergoes the punishment; other members of the community pray and do penance for his welfare until his release. *Karma* should not

be used to justify the happy time of one's self, nor for the condemnation of those who are deprived. Those who indulge in
this, which is quite opposite to the spirit of *Karma Siddhanta*
(the *Karma* doctrine), become sinners themselves – owing to
their indulgence in this, i.e. a wrong interpretation of *Karma*.

Islam

The concept of a prison or prisoner in the sense that we know
it today did not exist at the time of the Prophet Muhammad
(570–633 CE) (peace be upon him – *pbuh*). [The expression
pbuh is always repeated by Muslims when the Prophet is mentioned.] Yes, they had courts and judges, and yes, people were
caught for crimes, or gave themselves up voluntarily, but there
was no prison sentence, and there was no prison. However,
there was the *aseer* or prisoner of war (enemy soldiers or com-
batants who had been taken captive), and the *Qur'an* and the
Hadith (traditions of the Prophet) talk about their treatment:

> [The truly virtuous are] they [who] fulfil their vows, and
> stand in awe of a Day the woe of which is bound to
> spread far and wide,
> And who give food – however great be their own want of
> it – unto the needy, and the orphan, and the prisoner,
> [saying, in their hearts,] 'We feed you for the sake of God
> alone: we desire no recompense from you, nor thanks.'
>
> *Qur'an* 76:8–10

According to Zamakhshari and Razi, two of the earlier commentators of the Qur'an, the term aseer is extended to cover
'any rendered helpless', without freedoms, as the Prophet
(pbuh) once remarked: 'One who owes you money is your prisoner (i.e. helpless); be therefore, truly kind to your prisoner.'
What is also interesting is that many commentators give a wide
definition to 'food' to include food for the soul, welfare etc.
Indeed Huzayr ibn Humayr, an enemy combatant who fell into
Muslim hands, describes how he was staying with a Muslim
family after being captured. Whenever they had their meals,

they used to give him preference by offering him bread while they would eat only dates.

Hence offering care to the prisoners today would most definitely be recognised as a noble and Islamic activity. The Prophet (*pbuh*) said:

> The best of mankind (in the sight of God) is the one who benefits mankind most. (*Baihaqi*)
> God will aid the servant (of His) so long as the servant aids his brother. (*Muslim*)

Indeed Mercy, Love and Compassion figure much in Islamic traditions. When a man saw the Prophet (*pbuh*) kissing his grandson, he was astonished at the Prophet's action and said, 'I have ten children but I have never kissed any one of them.' The Prophet replied, 'He who does not show mercy, no mercy would be shown to him' (*Bukhari*).

Within the Islamic framework, we do not have a concept of a 'calling' as such, but we are driven to do the best we can for people. Why? Because it is we who need it. Often this concept of reciprocity or compensation for one's actions does not sit well with some of my Christian colleagues. The act of care and kindness that we do is for our own benefit. We believe it is God who has benevolently placed the opportunity in front of us to love and care for others, and how fortunate we are. The Prophet (*pbuh*) was told by the Angel Gabriel (*pbuh*): 'Woe to him who found his parents attaining old age and failed to enter Heaven' – in other words, he did not grasp the opportunity to care, to show compassion, to love.

In a similar fashion, our prison congregations are composed of people who are in pain; some have had limited access to love and kindness in their lives, or have been victims of society's ravages, or indeed of their own crimes. This is for many the most vulnerable time, as can be seen by the phenomenal rates of self-harm and suicide. Oscar Wilde (1854–1900), the Irish dramatist and poet, said during his incarceration in Reading Prison:

We who live in prison, and in whose lives there is no event but sorrow, have to measure time by throbs of pain, and the record of bitter moments.

Into this world has God thrust us, who like all *Bani Adam* (Children of Adam), are also vulnerable. But He has handed to us an opportunity to do the godly thing, to reflect the mercy of the Prophets.

It is we who 'minister' to prisoners that are actually the beneficiaries of our endeavours. It is we who need it. And what a privilege it is that He has granted us this opportunity. As he, the Prophet (*pbuh*), advised his companions:

> Those who have mercy will receive the mercy of the Most Merciful. Have mercy on those who are on earth, and the One in Heaven will have mercy on you. (*Tirmidhi*)
> Be kind, for whenever kindness becomes part of something, it beautifies it. Whenever it is taken from something, it leaves it tarnished. (*Bukhari*)

[Note: *Baihaqi, Muslim, Bukhari* and *Tirmidhi* are all books of *hadith* (sayings of the Prophet, *pbuh*).]

Sikhism

Recognise the human race as one!

The above words of Guru Gobind Singh, the tenth Guru of the Sikhs, form a central message of the Sikh Faith to all humanity. It is a message that echoes the teachings of Guru Nanak, the founder of Sikhism, who lived in the fifteenth century. This recognition of our common humanity sums up the ethos of Sikh Chaplains.

Guru Nanak preached that God is not influenced by the names of our different religions, or by the name we give to God, Jehovaha, or Allah. Sikhs believe that the true worship of God is in recognising the vibrant spirit of God in every person, and looking to the welfare of all, whatever their background or status in society. It is in the spirit of these teachings that Sikhs conclude their daily prayer with the words, '*Tere bhane Sarbat da bhalla*', a request to God to look to the wellbeing of all humanity.

Guru Nanak preached that true religion does not lie in empty rituals but in putting one's beliefs into practice for the welfare of others. Guru Nanak taught the concept of *gurmukh* and *manmukh* – free will that allows an individual to move in a positive or negative ethical direction. A person who has lived a life of selfishness or crime can move back to more purposeful living if he or she genuinely repents. A person who does not repent and closes his mind to truth and justice, removes himself further from an awareness of God that leads to social responsibility. The purpose of Sikh ministry is to help those who have been living in a negative way, to move back to *gurmukh* living and become real assets to society.

Positive or *gurmukh* living, according to Sikh teachings, requires us to live in three dimensions at one and the same time:

Nam Japna – loving God and meditating on attributes of God such as love, benevolence and kindness. A Sikh practises this to inculcate such virtues into his character.

Kirat Karni – a Sikh is advised to earn his livelihood by honest means. He is not supposed to be a parasite on society. A person's earnings, however large or small, should come from honest means. If a person is dishonest, and takes what is not justly his, the Gurus declare these earnings as the 'blood of the poor'. As such they are prohibited to a Sikh.

Vand ke chhakna – literally, 'sharing with others'. Sikh teachings emphasise sharing rather than giving. Giving suggests a moral superiority, with the recipient having a lower status. Some people broadcast the fact that they are contributing to the needy and feel proud of their image as benefactors. It is this pride (*ahankar*) which denies them the spiritual benefits obtained by a person who remains humble. Sikhs believe that God gives everything, including what we share with our fellow beings. We can't take credit for that. We give credit to God.

It is these principles of positive living that inform and inspire the work of Sikh Chaplains. We recognise that we are all capable of taking wrong turnings in life that can lead to negative living and social isolation. Sikhs believe it is the duty of all of us to help others get back on the path of positive living.

Judaism

Way back in 1966, I was appointed as cantor of the Hull Western Synagogue. I recall the communal rabbi telling us about his visits to HMP Hull to minister to the occasional Jewish prisoner detained there. I gave little thought to my senior colleague's prison work at the time, but things were to change dramatically some three years later, when I accepted a call to become cantor at the Brixton Synagogue, then a thriving congregation serving the Jewish community of South London. Soon after arriving in my new post, I received a call from the retiring minister of the Stanmore Synagogue who was the visiting rabbi at HMP Brixton and HMP Wandsworth. He was looking for someone to succeed him and thought that as I lived locally, I was eminently suitable to take over his chaplaincy at the two South London establishments. I thought to myself that there must surely be more important criteria in determining one's suitability for this important work. However, he suggested that I accompany him on his next visits, and I could then decide whether or not I was interested. I duly accepted his proposal and came away with a positive feeling that I would like to take on this responsibility and hopefully be able to make a useful contribution. Accordingly, and with little formality, I became the visiting rabbi at both prisons.

Looking back on those early years of my prison chaplaincy, I am shocked that I was thrown into the deep end, having received no training or induction and having no multi-faith chaplaincy team to support me. Yet somehow I found my way, notwithstanding the occasional *faux pas* due to naivety or plain ignorance of prison regulations. Thankfully, prison chaplaincy has come a long way since those days and is now an integral and highly professional department within every establishment. The quality of service it provides to prisoners and staff is truly beyond measure.

One element, however, has remained constant throughout the years, and that is the mission to provide for the religious and spiritual needs of prisoners in a totally non-judgemental manner. This is of particular importance to Jewish prisoners, who are few in number and may often experience a sense of loneliness and isolation. For them, the sight of a Jewish chaplain's friendly smile conveys an important and reassuring message that the Jewish community has not rejected them, regardless of the crimes they may have committed. In addition, religiously observant Jews will have specific needs to enable them to practise the laws of Judaism, and Jewish chaplains play a key role in ensuring that these needs are met within the framework of the prison regulations.

I am fortunate to lead a team of 40 dedicated Jewish chaplains who regularly visit Jewish prisoners throughout England and Wales. I take this opportunity to thank them for the outstanding work they do for Jewish prisoners on behalf of the United Synagogue Visitation Committee. It is also my privilege to serve as a member of the Chaplaincy Council, and I am ever grateful to the Chaplain General and council colleagues for their inspirational support and encouragement in our work, always within the spirit of mutual respect and cooperation.

In our daily prayers, we include the following words of praise to the Almighty:

> The beloved ones praise and exalt God and offer hymns, songs, praises, blessings and thanksgivings to the King, the living and enduring God who is exalted and uplifted, great and revered. He humbles the haughty and raises up the lowly; He leads forth the imprisoned, delivers the meek, helps the poor and answers those who cry out to Him.

May these words provide comfort and hope to those who have reached a low point in their lives, so that they will be inspired to move forward to better times in the future. Amen.

Prisons, prisoners and imprisoners

Andrew Coyle is Professor of Prison Studies in King's College London, and a former Prison Governor.

Comparative rates of imprisonment

In 2008 there are in excess of 9 million men, women and children in prison around the world. About half of these are held in prisons in the United States (2.3 million), China (1.6 million) and Russia (0.88 million).

Rates of imprisonment are usually quoted per 100,000 of the total population. On that basis, the world rate of imprisonment is about 140. Prison population rates vary considerably between different regions of the world and also between different parts of the same continent. For example, the rate for West African countries is 52 per 100,000 whereas for Southern African countries it is 324. The rate for South Central Asian countries (mainly the Indian sub-continent) is 55, whereas for Central Asian countries it is 386. The rate for Southern European countries is 80 whereas for Central and Eastern European countries it is 184 per 100,000.

It is interesting to compare rates of imprisonment between some neighbouring countries. The United States, with something less than 5 per cent of the population of the world, has almost 25 per cent of the world's prisoners. Its rate of imprisonment is 751 per 100,000. This is in contrast to its northern neighbour, Canada, which has a rate of 108. The rate of imprisonment in Spain is 149, while that in France is 91. Denmark has a rate of 66, compared to 117 in the Netherlands. Finland, which has a population slightly larger than Scotland's, has a rate of 68, compared to the Scottish 139.

How are we to explain these gross disparities between

otherwise similar countries? Some commentators attempt to do so by reference to crime rates, but this is a notoriously difficult exercise because of the wide range of variables, including the way data is collected and the way crime is defined in different countries. The EU points out in its statistical crime bulletin that 'comparisons of crime levels based on the absolute figures would be misleading … direct comparisons of crime levels in different countries should be avoided.' It is also difficult to explain changes in imprisonment rates by reference to changes in crime rates, as the following table from a Home Office publication shows:

Changes in imprisonment rates and recorded crime rates for selected states between 1991 and 2001

State	Crime rate	Prison rate
Canada	-17%	+2%
Denmark	-9%	-9%
England and Wales	-11%	+45%
Netherlands	+13%	+105%
Spain	+3%	+28%

There is virtually no evidence from any country that high or low rates of imprisonment reflect high or low crime rates.

One explanation for differing rates of imprisonment among countries came from a somewhat unusual source. In November 2002 the heads of prison administrations in all the countries of the Council of Europe met in Strasbourg. In their final communiqué they noted that levels of imprisonment rarely have anything to do with levels of crime. Instead, they are a matter of political and public choice. The heads of prison administration suggested that a society could choose to have a high or a low level of imprisonment, depending on what sort of society it wished to be.

If it is true that a society can choose how many of its citizens it wishes to imprison, it is worth spending a moment to consider who are these people who are sent to prison. For a start, they will include those who have been convicted of serious crimes or who are a genuine threat to public safety. There is rarely any dispute in any country that such people should be in prison. People who have committed murder, serious physical assault or serious sexual offences are invariably sent to prison. Countries may differ in the length of sentence passed on such people, but there will be little doubt that they will receive a prison sentence.

However, in many countries these groups do not constitute the majority of prisoners. Prison numbers are swelled by the mentally ill, by drug addicts and by social misfits. It is a truism to say that if one wishes to know which are the marginalised groups in any country, one only has to look in its prisons, where they will invariably be over-represented: the Roma in Hungary and the Czech Republic, the aboriginals in Australia, the Maori in New Zealand, black and Hispanic people in the United States. The United Kingdom is not immune from this phenomenon. When considering all of these factors, we might also bear in mind the injunction of Nelson Mandela: 'A nation should be judged not by how it treats its highest citizens, but its lowest ones.'

The consequences of increased numbers of prisoners

In Judicial Unit 40, a detention centre in Bogota, Colombia, cells are often so full that prisoners are forced to lie on top of each other, with up to 19 prisoners crammed into cells designed to hold 4. The Modelo Prison is the main pre-trial prison for Bogota. It has a capacity for 1500 prisoners. When I visited several years ago, it held 3450 male prisoners. At any one time there were about 150 guards on duty to look after these men – a hopelessly inadequate number to effect proper supervision. Most of the guards were in their late teens and serving their year of compulsory national service. The prisoners were held in 5 large accommodation blocks built around patios. The guards did not usually go inside these patios. In each of the units there was a prisoner nominated as 'monitor'. This in effect meant that prisoners had developed their own rules and regulations for running the patios. Prisoners who could not pay or who did not have influence with the leading prisoners were likely to fare very badly.

The effects of overcrowding in some prisons in Russia are difficult to describe. Addressing a parliamentary hearing in Moscow in 1995, the Head of the General Penitentiary Department said:

> I have to confess that sometimes official reports on prisoners' deaths do not convey the real facts. In reality, prisoners die from overcrowding, lack of oxygen and poor prison conditions ... Cases of death from lack of oxygen took place in almost all large pre-trial detention centres in Russia ... The critical situation ... is deteriorating day by day: the prison population grows on average by 3,500 to 4,000 inmates a month.

Following a visit to the Butyrskaya and Matrosskaya pre-trial prisons in Moscow around this time, the UN Special Rapporteur on Torture reported:

> The Special Rapporteur would need the poetic skills of a Dante or the artistic skills of a Bosch adequately to describe the infernal conditions he found in these cells.

Some of the worst prison conditions are to be found in countries which are former colonies. The Nigerian Civil Liberties Organisation has reported significant overcrowding in most of the country's prisons. A prisoner in Zaria Prison described what this overcrowding meant in practice:

> We have three batches in my cell, and I am in Number Two. Other cells have four, even five, when there are many prisoners. When it is time to sleep, we all make space for the first batch. We stand at one end of the cell, or sit. Some of us sleep while standing, but you do not lie down. Only the first batch lies down. After four hours,

they get up, and we lie down to sleep. After four hours, we
get up, and the third batch will sleep.

The pressures of overcrowding in England and Wales have not
yet reached the levels experienced in Colombia, Russia or
Nigeria, but they have been increasing inexorably in recent
years, and one can take scant comfort from the comment of the
Secretary of State for Justice after a visit to prisons in the
United States in February 2008, that he did not intend 'to com-
promise the safety of staff and prisoners by following the
American example of turning gyms into mass dormitories'.

    There are two main responses to prison overcrowding. The
first is simply to build more prisons and to provide more
spaces. No jurisdiction in the world has ever built its way out
of prison overcrowding. Sir Alexander Paterson, a famous
English Prison Commissioner in the early twentieth century
and a man of many aphorisms, explained this with his comment, 'Wherever prisons are built, the courts will fill them.' The
second response is to restrict the use of prison as punishment
for those who have committed the most serious crimes or who
are a genuine threat to public safety, while at the same time
finding other ways of dealing with what are primarily matters
of social justice.

A narrow role for criminal justice

The criminal justice process has a very narrow role to play in
creating and nurturing a safe and just society. In recent years
we have allowed criminal justice to expand into areas where it
has no locus. Criminal justice systems can be used to underpin
and to help to support the values of a society. They cannot be
used as a substitute for these values.

    In 1995 an amazing conference took place in Kampala on
the subject of penal reform in Africa. In opening that conference, William Omaria, the Ugandan Minister of the Interior,
referred to imprisonment as follows:

    One day in the distant future, people will probably look

back on what happens in most countries today and will wonder how we could do that to our fellow human beings in the name of justice.

Our hope should be that that day will not be too long in coming.

Information
Regularly updated data on prisons can be sourced at www.prisonstudies.org

PRISON LIFE

Reception

Each year in the UK, about 130,000 people are received into prison custody for the first time. Each one will react to the transition in slightly different ways, but the central experience is similar for all. The following two accounts of the process (one written by a former prisoner) convey something of the emotions that are aroused. Many prisons have 'first night in custody' suites, where some of the best of the prison staff seek to ameliorate the negative effects of this difficult experience. They work with other colleagues, and frequently with prisoners, some trained as Listeners, to help ease the transition from freedom to imprisonment. For a small number of prisoners there is relief at being imprisoned – an ironic escape from the chaotic lifestyle that brings about imprisonment.

Fred Taylor was 63 years of age when I met him in the Prison Health Centre. Though not a Christian, he had asked to see me.

'I never believed I would ever experience anything like it,' he said. 'It was awful.'

When he had entered the prison, the Reception Officer had asked him, 'Who are you?'

'Mr Taylor,' he had replied automatically, but with uncertainty. Suddenly he had felt bewildered, anxious and isolated. At that moment he had really felt the full force of being 'inside'.

Fred described the way in which his few possessions had been searched, his wallet emptied, the photographs of his wife and children almost carelessly handled, he felt. That simple action had caused him deep pain.

As we talked, he reflected on his time in police cells, in the van bringing him to prison, known as 'the sweat-box'. When it had entered the first of the prison gates, the engine had been

turned off whilst it was security checked and the appropriate
paperwork about its 'contents' was given to the Gate Officer.
Before it re-started and before it entered the inner gates, Fred
said his heart had raced as he viewed razor-wire and high
fences from the tiny window of the van. He had asked himself,
'When will I next go out?'

He had never been in prison before and now he was being
'processed', subjected to a 'strip-search', which he saw as the
final humiliation as he was 'dehumanised', stripped of his
dignity. 'I felt as if I was being mocked,' he said, 'though no one
said a word wrong. The whole procedure just seemed designed
to humiliate me. I know it's the system but it's awful. And then,
I was given a phone call to my wife, barely remembered in
subsequent days, but a moment of normality, with some
reassurance.'

> After mocking him, they stripped him of the robe and
> put his own clothes on him.
>
> Matthew 27:31a

Crucified God,
you know what it is to be mocked,
to be stripped and vulnerable.
Be with those who
enter prison for the first time today.
Be present in their vulnerability
and in those who have care of them.
In this vulnerability may they
know their worth in your eyes.
In their anxiety and uncertainty
may they know that your Son has
shared their experience and
transformed it.

*

I had a letter from Jean, a former prisoner, in which she described
the sense of loss of identity which she experienced on entering the

prison system. She also wrote of the healing which subsequently
took place and of the eventual knowledge of God's love and
acceptance of her. She wrote:

I can remember the lack of emotion that surrounded me on
entering the reception area of the Prison, the expressionless
faces and hard voices that 'greeted' me at a time when I most
needed to feel acceptance, understanding and warmth. Up
until then I had not been so much aware of the 'universal'
rejection of me as a person, but this realisation was a hard
revelation of the fact that I, from that moment, had ceased to
be a person. I had become a number, a number that would be
etched in my memory forever.

'Go into the cubicle and take off your clothes,' I was
instructed by one of the duty reception officers. 'You can put
on the dressing-gown there, and call us when you're ready.'

Without feeling, I followed the instructions. The dressing-
gown was rough and cold, but as it had no belt with which to
tie it, I wrapped it tightly around myself, waiting for what was
to come next.

The officer came right up close to me and said, 'Open your
mouth.'

As I did this, she felt through my hair and then looked into
my mouth. 'Right,' she said, 'pick up your clothes and follow
me.'

I followed the officer into a well-lit room, furnished with a
large desk, filing cabinets and weighing scales. Two large chairs
were situated at either end of the desk.

'What is your name? Date of birth? Your religion? Your
nationality? What are you charged with?' – and many more
questions. I answered without thinking, as if it really wasn't me
who was speaking.

And then I was told, 'Your number is PN46570. You must
remember that number. You will have it as long as you are in
this prison and you will be identified by it throughout the
prison.'

And the photograph, with that number on it, had a major

impact on me. *Who am I?*, I thought. *Am I really this criminal, this nobody?*

Having had a bath, I was led to my cell and the door slammed shut behind me. Alone and afraid, I thought some more. *Am I really who they say I am? Why can't I remember the person I thought I was? I don't know who I am any more.*

I really continued in this 'zombie' state for some time, searching for answers, which, I was to discover, only God could provide.

Over time, and in my emptiness, I turned to the God from whom I had turned away for so long. I knew he could hear me, that he was listening, and whilst there was no 'flash of lightning', no 'instant change', I knew God had welcomed me to him. There, in the stillness, I began to learn of the person God intended me to be rather than the person I thought I should be. Never before had I been so much aware of the fact that I was a Child of God, chosen by him, and that it was only through my ignorance, my selfishness that I had chosen to deny him.

> O Lord, you have searched me out and known me.
> Where can I go from your Spirit?
> How weighty are your thoughts, O God!
> How vast is the sum of them!
> I try to count them – they are more than sand;
> I come to the end – I am still with you.
>
> Psalm 139:1, 7, 17–18

> For you did not receive a spirit of slavery to fall back into fear, but you have received a spirit of adoption. When we cry, 'Abba! Father!' it is that very Spirit bearing witness with our spirit that we are children of God, and if children, then heirs, heirs of God and joint heirs with Christ – if, in fact, we suffer with him so that we may also be glorified with him. I consider that the sufferings of this present time are not worth comparing with the glory about to be revealed to us.
>
> Romans 8:15–18

Jean's prayer:

> *Ever living, ever loving Lord,*
> *your mercy to me, love for me and knowledge of me*
> *are too great for me to understand.*
> *But your promises that you will hear us*
> *when we cry out to you*
> *are so true.*
> *I thank you that you are always there,*
> *ready to reach out to us*
> *in a way that only you can.*
> *May we come to know you more and more,*
> *to know of your wonderful plans*
> *for our lives, and by this*
> *may we truly come to be new creations,*
> *seeking to do your will, rather than our own.*
> *Lord, in your name we pray.*
> *Amen.*

Jean is now a Pastoral Assistant in a parish.

Separation

Eric sat with a cup of coffee in his hand, dejected. The realisation of the consequences of his offence, its effect on his family, had begun to hit him, and he had sought a place of refuge in the quiet of the Chapel.

Unlike an estimated 45 per cent of male prisoners who had lost their partners since the start of their prison sentence, Eric still had the support of his wife and children. Perhaps, not surprisingly, some 59 per cent of male prisoners, and 66 per cent of females, have children under the age of 18, with as many as 160,000 children experiencing the imprisonment of a parent in any year. As many as 40 per cent of fathers serving sentences receive no visits from their children. Sometimes, of course, the truth of the situation is kept from children, to protect them, and as part of a coping mechanism by some parents.

Eric's acknowledgement to me, and to his family, of his guilt, had caused him much embarrassment. He could see in his wife and children their embarrassment and the feelings of conflict which they experienced on entering the visits room. Joy at being with Eric, shame at being in such a place.

In conversation, he said, 'I knew what I was doing, but I never realised the effect it would have on those I love.' Eric's wife and children were innocent victims of his actions, and of a system in which innocent and guilty are punished alike. The now popular refrain, 'If you can't do the time, don't do the crime', ignores and trivialises the devastation which comes to many families, and it ignores the centrality of relationships, impinging on the future of all concerned. Too many become scapegoats in their communities and relationships may break under the strain. Children, lacking the stability which they need, may suffer emotional damage, providing a basis for future behavioural problems, and potentially, for entry into crime or delinquency. Resentment, mistrust and fear of authority are almost inevitable, for some.

Eric, six months on, finds himself still 'trying to explain myself to my family, always apologising, and always fearful I will lose them. Sometimes I find visits so hard that it would be better not to have them at all – the emotional trauma, concentrated into one hour, three times a month, is unbelievable – it takes days to get over them ... God knows what it's doing to my wife and children.'

I have known some prisoners, particularly those imprisoned for 'life', who have found the burden of guilt and separation so intense that they have broken family ties, in the hope of coping more easily with their time inside. Such a decision involves enormous 'cost' for them and for their families. A former Home Secretary stressed the importance of maintaining relationships:

> As we consider the practical steps intended to equip offenders with the means to avoid re-offending we also need to remember the vital role of family, friends and community. I believe that we sometimes fail to give enough emphasis to the powerful impact of supportive relationships to prisoners – to realise that offenders often care deeply about letting down those closest to them, and want to show that they can change, but somehow just never get there. An offender is much less likely to re-offend if he feels part of a family and community, from which he receives support as well as owes obligations.

Release and re-integration can also be a traumatic time, and without the right form of support, all too many re-offend. Research has shown that maintaining family contact increases the chance of successful resettlement.

> *God of love,*
> *the pain of separation*
> *often overwhelms*

and is destructive.
We hold in your presence
all who are separated
in mind or body from
those whom they love,
and especially the 'innocent victims'
of imprisonment, the families,
friends and relatives of prisoners.
We acknowledge before you
the importance of relationships,
with one another,
and with you.
Enable us to pursue them,
for their good,
and in response
to your pursuit of us.

Waiting

'I'm celebrating an anniversary today, Chaplain,' said the prisoner as I walked past him.

I stopped. 'What's that for, then, Nick?' I asked.

'I've been here a year today.'

I could hardly believe it. For me, his time had seemed to pass so quickly. 'When's your trial?' I asked.

Despondently, he gave me a date five months in the future. 'Yeah, I'll have done 17 months before I even get into court.'

He went on to express his anger and frustration with a judicial system which was moving so slowly and in the process was causing him deep distress, anxiety and uncertainty. And for his family as well. He was contemplating taking some form of action to highlight his situation and he wanted to know if I felt hunger-strike would be a way of bringing his case to the fore. I tried to dissuade him on the grounds that he would ultimately hurt only himself and his family.

'I don't care,' he said. 'I'm dying inside anyway.'

The year had certainly taken its toll. His appearance had altered. His complexion was sallow, as he had had little time in the fresh air and sunlight. His eyes were deep within their sockets. His face was unshaven and his voice flat. He had been waiting for twelve long months. Now he knew another five had to be endured. No words of mine could help Nick. To have spoken about the spirituality of waiting, or the need for 'patience', would have been to insult him.

Some weeks before, in the prison car-park, I had met Pete. He had been released from court on the second day of his trial. He had waited one year and two days on remand. In court, his case was dismissed by the trial judge, who said it should never have come to court. In the car-park, Pete spoke movingly of his 'waiting', and of what he had lost: his wife, his children, his home, his business. Because of a conviction some years before, he would not be eligible for compensation. His bitterness was understandable. His determination to rebuild his broken life admirable.

Such lengthy periods of time spent waiting on remand are rare, but not exceptional. It is hard to see how they can further the cause of justice.

> Therefore justice is far from us,
> and righteousness does not reach us;
> we wait for light, and lo! there is darkness;
> and for brightness, but we walk in gloom.
>
> Isaiah 59:9

> *God of justice,*
> *help us to be alert*
> *to your presence*
> *in our lives.*
> *Help us to understand*
> *that waiting is not passive,*
> *but active and open-ended.*
> *We pray for patience,*
> *for the ability*
> *to stay where we are,*
> *to live each situation to the full*
> *in the belief that something hidden*
> *will be revealed to us.*
> *We hold before you those*
> *who are impatient*
> *and always expecting*
> *the real thing to happen somewhere else.*
> *May we dare to stay where we are,*
> *that we may know your presence*
> *in the present moment.*

Bargaining

The phone call was from a solicitor. Could Tom attend court the following Friday to speak for Roger? He had, after all, undergone a conversion experience. I explained that members of the Chaplaincy Team rarely attended court to speak in this way. We would be inundated with requests, particularly if people felt that 'a result' would be helped by our presence. In this context 'a result' means a positive outcome for the accused. I said 'No', it was not our policy, as a Team, to do so.

A few hours later an eloquent barrister phoned. He understood all that had been said to the solicitor, but ... he was sure that his client had undergone a life-changing experience and that the Judge should be made aware of the difference between the youth (he was just 18) who had committed the offence some months before, and the 'born-again Christian', now transformed.

My colleague, a young volunteer, who was leaving us two weeks later, decided to 'break ranks' and to appear in court. He spoke on Roger's behalf, eloquently and with passion.

Two days later I was on the Wing, and I asked staff members if there was anyone who wanted to attend chapel. I mentioned Roger. 'He hasn't asked,' said one. I was surprised – he had been so regular an attender, Sunday and Thursday. 'He's had a bit of bad news this week,' said another. 'Might be no harm if you saw him.'

I knocked on his cell door, opened it and was faced with a young man who would not speak to me, made it clear I should leave, and rejected my presence.

Was he rejecting me as a person, as a chaplain, as a father figure, or the God whom he felt had let him down in court? He had been given a four-and-a-half-year sentence. I was reminded of when my son was young. He sometimes rejected me when

he did not get what he asked for. It was usually temporary.
Perhaps for Roger too.

> *Lord,*
> *we all try it,*
> *to do deals with you.*
> *To think belief is*
> *a 'quid pro quo'.*
> *Help us not to*
> *minimise your love*
> *by reducing it to our understanding.*
> *Help us to know your love*
> *for its own sake.*

Space

One of the foremost prison architects of the eighteenth century, William Blackburn, believed that the design of prisons could help prisoners to learn self-control and rational behaviour, leading in turn to a reshaping of human nature. The concept of the monastic cell, in which the prisoner could contemplate his offence before God, seek forgiveness and repentance, was strong. Monks may well have found their cells a place of contemplation, but for a prisoner it is simply a place of confinement.

Today such a concept is meaningless for the vast majority of prisoners, and the sense of isolation imposed by a 'single' cell may do harm to some people if they are unsuited to it psychologically.

Most cells are about 3.60m by 2.75m and designed for one person. Many will be shared by two people, two chairs, a small table, two lockers, a washbasin and a toilet. A small window, two metres from the ground, gives some natural light and some air – though little when the door is closed, especially in summer. There is little 'personal' space in such a cell, in which meals must also be eaten and leisure activities indulged.

It is both 'personal' space and 'public', for there is constant intrusion during the day – officers locking and unlocking, other prisoners in and out, probation staff, chaplaincy staff, and perhaps a search team checking security, looking for illegally held items, including drugs. And just occasionally, and unannounced, a 'sniffer' dog helping the search teams. Ever present too, is the observation panel in the cell door – the 'spy-hole', the 'eye in the door'.

In such a place, the opportunity to respect personal space is limited. But it can be done, to a limited extent. Whenever I or one of my colleagues is going to a cell, and despite our carrying cell keys, we will always knock on the door before inserting the key, and when we open the door, will always ask, 'May I come in?' It is the prisoner's 'home', their 'pad', for however short or long a period that might be.

> *Lord God,*
> *your Son sought space*
> *to find himself, and you;*
> *space for re-generation*
> *and re-creation; help us*
> *respect the need for space*
> *necessary for each individual's growth.*
> *Help us to encounter*
> *and engage you in that space.*

Victimisation

I have rarely seen violence perpetrated in my time in prison. I have seen the consequences – the death (mercifully, rare), maiming and scarring, physical and mental, of prisoners and staff. As I sat with Graham, who could only explain the attack as being racially motivated, he showed me the stitches in his skull, caused by a common prison weapon – a battery, a tin can or some other heavy object placed in a sock and then swung at the victim from behind and usually aimed at the head. People can be threatened, and intimidation is a significant factor for some.

Over 1000 incidents of serious assault are recorded each year. A violence-reduction strategy encourages staff and prisoners to report all incidents. The more common forms of victimising behaviour are assault, threat of violence, robbery, verbal abuse/insult, theft, and exclusion from activities.

It is, perhaps, understandable that such incidents foster a sense of anxiety for some. In response to this problem of victimisation/bullying in prison, the violence-reduction strategy helps staff to measure the extent of the problem and to change attitudes to it. It also seeks to provide improved supervision and detection of the problem, and to support victims; and to challenge the victimisers to face up to their antisocial behaviour and to change.

Against such a background, it could become easy to assume that force, and more particularly, violence, is the only effective response. This sentiment, so often reflected in some parts of the media, and seeming only to condemn offenders, is at variance with Christian thinking. Christians working and ministering in such an environment have to hold before them the theological possibility of forgiveness in a world where God's grace seems, so often, to be absent. They must also seek alternative models. As part of the Safer Prisons initiative, many prisons have a Safer Prison Co-ordinator, part of whose task is to oversee the anti-bullying strategy, working with staff and prisoners to create a community that is safe and respectful.

Why do you make me see wrongdoing and look at trouble? Destruction and violence are before me; strife and contention arise.

Habakkuk 1:3

Lord of life,
in the midst of a violent world,
help us to seek for
an alternative way;
to seek for the way
of peace and reconciliation
which brings about the transformation
of broken lives.

We hold before you
victimisers who are victims,
broken people who
want to break others,
sad people whose sadness
is in their actions.

Be present in the words
and actions of those
who seek alternatives;
and as we learn
to embody forgiveness,
we acknowledge our
brokenness before you.

Drugs

It is believed that up to 55 per cent of people entering prisons have a serious drug misuse problem, with some local prisons reporting 80 per cent of entrants testing positive for class A drugs.

Random drug testing was introduced in 1995. All prisoners are subject to this test. About 10.3 per cent of those tests are positive, according to the 'Drugs: Our Community, Your Say' consultation paper, based on figures from 2005/6. But a report by the Office for National Statistics has found that, although they are a statistically valid indicator of drug trends, random test results underestimate the level of drug misuse as reported by prisoners.

Charlie has been tested. He was the last of seven children, but one too many. At two years of age he was in a children's home (over 23 per cent of prisoners have been in some form of local authority care, based on figures issued by the Courts Service in 2007).

He thinks he was about 13 or 14 before he saw his mother again. At about that time he went to live with his father and step-mother. Relationships were strained and within a short time he was involved in petty crime, which escalated over a few years, culminating with a sentence in a Detention Centre (now called Young Offender Institutions).

He was introduced to a 'spliff' – a joint or reefer of cannabis. Unlike many others, Charlie believes that cannabis can lead to harder drugs and that few people are likely to start drugs by using heroin or crack-cocaine.

On release from the Detention Centre, he got heavily involved in the 'rave' scene, where the music, the atmosphere and the incredible 'buzz' which drugs gave, enhanced every experience. Ecstasy, at about £15 a tablet at that time, soon gave

way to the highly addictive crack-cocaine, at about £20 a 'rock'
– a piece about one-fifth of the size of a small, round mint. On
average he spent £300–£400 each week, sometimes £1000.

Burglary and theft paid for this habit, and when he was
eventually caught, he got a three-year sentence. Aged 25, he
began to wonder about the direction of his life, and he took no
further drugs in prison.

Eighteen months later he was on the streets again, penniless,
homeless, and 'lost'. Within days he was robbing, within weeks
back on hard drugs. He bought a car, rented a flat, gambled
more, increased his drug intake, and his dependency. The hap-
piness he sought continued to evade him. Within months he
was back in prison, depressed and determined to leave drugs
aside.

An interest in religion stemming from his time in the
children's home led him to chapel. He acknowledged the mess
he was in, the physical and mental anguish which led to him
crying himself to sleep for three months, as he 'rocked' himself
on his bed. He started reading the Bible and was eventually
baptised. He arranged to go to a Rehabilitation Clinic if he got
a non-custodial sentence. He did not, and he went down for
two years. Moved to another prison, he was quickly involved in
supplying heroin and crack-cocaine. He started to 'use' once
more.

Released again, he decided to put his past behind him and a
relative gave him a job, learning to fit windows. 'A bit rich, that,
really, given that I was more used to removing them!' It was
irregular work, with low pay, which led to him feeling he was
going nowhere. He sought for alternative work, 'But the more
I knocked, the more doors were closed.' His relationship with
his girlfriend was a mess. In the midst of it all, he sought out a
priest, who talked with him, listened to him, and said, 'You
know what you have to do. Do it!'

The work stopped, and the bills mounted. On his way to pay
for crack-cocaine, he crashed his girlfriend's car, causing £4000
worth of damage. In despair, he spent the last £40 of the house-
keeping money on crack. Fearing the response of his girlfriend,

he burgled, and was caught. A day later, he arrived in the prison where I met him.

Within a short time he stood on a chair in his cell, with one end of a strip of sheet tied to one of the window bars, the other end tied around his neck. A quarter of an hour passed. The despair and isolation which he had felt slowly began to pass. Strength came from somewhere, and a sense of 'calm' entered him. There could be 'no bargains, no promises, just me and what I want to do', he thought.

Now, Charlie has changed. No longer, it seems, does he say to God, 'Here I am – let's hear what you've got to say', with the expectation of receiving instant answers. Trying again, he has got another place in a different Rehabilitation Clinic. He feels his life is no longer at a crossroads, but facing a one-way street, whose direction he must take. He is, he says, 'more focused, and prison can teach me no more'. He is reading his Bible again, but less intently. As he waits for trial, he knows he will not be one of the positive drug-test results.

Over 8000 prisoners complete intensive drug rehabilitation programmes during the course of a year. Additionally, nearly 60,000 entered clinical services (i.e. detoxification or maintenance prescribing) in 2007/8 and over 73,000 received initial assessments through CARATs (Counselling, Assessment, Referral, Advice and Through-care services) or YPSMS (Young People's Substance Misuse Services). But not all who have a problem want help.

> *God of freedom,*
> *we hold before you*
> *all who are imprisoned by addiction*
> *and for whom life has*
> *no meaning except in illusion.*
>
> *God of freedom,*
> *help them to overcome*
> *the fear of self*
> *which holds them hostage.*

God of freedom,
who sent your Son
to set us free,
strengthen them
by your Spirit
that they may be able
to seek new directions,
be helped to work for their freedom.

Many of those with whom I have contact never find that freedom of which the prayer speaks. Mickey was 27 years old when we first met. He had used drugs for nearly 15 years. He regularly came and went from prison, and often said he would not live until he was 30. The last time we spoke, he had inherited some money, and a new start was predicted as he left, yet again. Within weeks he was dead, from an overdose. Shortly afterwards another two ex-prisoners were also dead, from overdoses. Not all will be able to change direction.

God of compassion,
we entrust to your care
those who have died
as slaves to addiction.
In your mercy,
grant them rest.
And in our failing them,
release us.

Brokenness

'Are you High Church?' came the question as I arrived in the Health Centre to lead the Sunday worship. I tried to explain that prison chaplains really should be 'Broad Church', to be flexible and responsive to people's needs, not seeking to impose a personal, predetermined churchmanship on those in chapel.

I enquired about his church background, to be told he had been on the Parochial Church Council, the Deanery Synod and the Diocesan Synod in his home area. In chapel, where it is usually difficult to get men to name one hymn they might like to sing, he could name many, and the names of the tunes! Robust and vocal in the early part of the service, he read the lesson with confidence.

In the prayers I noticed the movement of his hand as he wiped away the tears. At the Peace, he seemed less confident. During the Eucharistic prayer the tears continued, intermittently.

At the invitation to Communion, I adapted and used some words written by an American liturgist:

> My brothers, I invite you to bring your lives, in their brokenness and incompleteness, but wholly acceptable to God; that he, in this Eucharist might take your life, transform it and give it back to you made whole, transformed with his love.

The tears became more evident as the power of these words, the work of the Holy Spirit, and the turbulent emotions he was experiencing, combined in a deeply meaningful way for Mike. Afterwards, composed once more, he was subdued and reflective, more in touch with his emotions, and with God.

Broken bread has become a very significant symbol in our

Christian liturgy. In its symbolism there is a deep sacramental meaning which concerns the acceptance of our brokenness before, and by God. At a more fundamental level, it is about the simple sharing of food and drink, the one communal meal in many prisons, where most people eat alone.

In eating broken bread, in drinking wine, we try to become like Jesus, to obey his word and to follow him. Perhaps Mike was rediscovering his calling through the acceptance offered by God, manifest in the Eucharist.

> For I was hungry and you gave me food. I was thirsty and you gave me something to drink, I was a stranger and you welcomed me, I was naked and you gave me clothing, I was sick and you took care of me, I was in prison and you visited me.
>
> Matthew 25:35

Lord, in our brokenness
we receive your broken body in Christ;
broken on the Cross
and repeatedly in the Eucharist.
Take our lives
shattered by experience,
and in transforming them,
help to make them whole.
Enfold us in your light and power
that your will may be done.

Time

For six months I had responsibility for the chaplaincy in a women's prison, just a few miles from Wakefield Prison, where I was the Anglican Chaplain. Twice a week, and every third Sunday, I left the high-security environment and went to New Hall Women's Prison. At the beginning of 2008 women were held in 14 prisons in England, but there were no women prisoners in Wales. Within a total prison population of over 83,000, some 4510 are women. In the last ten years the women's population has doubled. Almost a thousand women are foreign nationals. Almost 60 per cent of women had used drugs on a daily basis before imprisonment. In one study, 78 per cent of women indicated psychological disturbance on admission to prison – compared to 15 per cent in the general adult female population.

New Hall was then a small prison, with just over 100 prisoners. It has continued to grow to nearly 400. It also has a mother-and-baby unit. It was, and is, a busy prison with a high turnover of prisoners (nearly 66 per cent of women are sentenced to custody for six months, or less). They have difficult stories to tell, of sexual and physical abuse, of drug addiction, petty theft, psychological disturbance, and prostitution. The number of women in prison who pose a threat to the public is very small.

Jan's story was not typical. She had come from a comfortable, protected background. In all, she was in prison for nearly eight years. Nothing, she said, could have prepared her for her first experience of prison. Facing a long sentence, she expressed feelings of being desperate, hopeless and lonely, combined with guilt and self-hatred for the pain which she had caused.

Jan sometimes remarked that there were so many others around her who were like her that they never shared their feelings. 'Each one of us,' she said, 'was trapped in our own prison, within the prison around us.'

Jan was not able to share the depth of her guilt, feeling nobody would understand. There had been heavy media coverage of her trial and some hostility when she first entered prison.

As time passed, she came to terms with everyday life in prison, and with what had happened in her life. She had plenty of time to think, to reflect on a life which seemed to be going nowhere.

It was in that time that Jan eventually decided 'to reach out to God', and in doing so she realised the significance of Christ's life and death. It was a slow process, a gradual conversion, but it became the 'most painful and joyous moment of my life', she said when we spoke in the chapel after worship. We had sung the hymn 'Do not be afraid', with its chorus:

> Do not be afraid, for I have redeemed you.
> I have called you by your name; you are mine.

For Jan, it gave expression to everything which years of imprisonment, physical and spiritual, had denied her.

> But now thus says the Lord,
> he who created you, O Jacob,
> he who formed you, O Israel:
> Do not fear, for I have redeemed you;
> I have called you by name, you are mine.
> When you pass through the waters,
> I will be with you;
> and through the rivers, they shall
> not overwhelm you;
> when you walk through fire
> you shall not be burned,
> and the flame shall not consume you ...
> Because you are precious in my sight,
> and honoured, and I love you.

Isaiah 43:1–2, 4a

Loving God,
we give you thanks
that you have redeemed us
through your love.
Help us to realise that in the midst
of our loneliness and anxiety,
you are at our side.
We acknowledge your presence
and your call which comes
when we listen for your voice.
We rejoice that we are
your people and you our God.

Information

In June 2008 a National Framework for Women Offenders was launched. It sets out the government's strategy for addressing the specific needs of female offenders, ensuring that they have the same opportunities as male offenders. For further information, visit: www.justice.gov.uk/news

Sentenced

'The Face of Evil', proclaimed the front page of one tabloid newspaper. 'Kinky killer', another. Each accompanied by photographs. 'Girl's killer gets life', was the more restrained heading on the inside page of a broadsheet. Standing in Sainsbury's, I briefly glanced through each paper. Significant words leapt from the pages, each one powerful in its condemnation of a woman who had murdered.

This was the same woman with whom I had sat the previous Sunday. And with whom I had prayed.

Now, she was starting a life sentence, and I was confused. Confused by what I had read, which seemed so at variance with *who* I had encountered. Some words from William Trevor's powerful novel, *Felicia's Journey*, kept ringing in my ears: 'Lost within a man who murdered, there was a soul like any other soul, purity itself it surely once had been.'[11]

As we had spoken, I had glimpsed something of that 'lost soul', and in so doing I had acknowledged how damaged it was, and yet how God seemed present and active because of that, and not despite it. I could not begin to understand why she had committed the crime, but I tried to begin the process of understanding the person who had done so, through listening, encounter and dialogue.

As I left her, I knew she would get 'Life'. Now, in Sainsbury's, the tabloid newspapers seemed to assault her dignity, and mine. And yet, I was left with a feeling that God, the God of compassion and forgiveness, continues to offer a release from our darkness, and can indeed provide the hope of reconciliation and new life, even in the face of sin.

> *God, whose face*
> *is that of love,*

be with those
who have recently
been sentenced.
In their uncertainty
and in their despair,
be present.
Enable their release
from darkness,
and through reconciliation and hope,
enable them to seek
new life and restoration
in you.

We pray for those
involved in the media,
for their responsibility
in reporting news;
that they may do so
having regard for the value
of each person.

Doing life

In March 2008, there were almost 11,000 people serving life, or indeterminate sentences, in England and Wales – an increase of over 30 per cent on the previous year. Around 9900 are male, 330 are female, and 775 are young offenders.

The average time served by life-sentence prisoners first released on licence has gradually increased from 10.7 years in 1985 to 14 years in 2005. It must be remembered that this 'average' relates only to those who have been released, and they represent a small proportion of 'lifers'. There are many who have served between 15 and 35 years.

On average, some 1650 people released after serving an indeterminate sentence are under active supervision by the Probation Service. Each of these is on licence. 'On licence' means an offender may be returned to prison automatically if he/she breaks the law, or even shows any cause for concern to the supervising Probation Officer, such as a change in personality or behaviour, alcohol or drug abuse, or showing signs of repeating the circumstances which may have led to the original offence. Any reasonable cause for concern which may be considered a risk to the public could result in the lifer being returned to prison. A life licence remains in force for the rest of the individual's life. Those offenders released on licence after serving a sentence of Imprisonment for Public Protection (IPP) can apply to have their licence terminated after ten years by the Parole Board, and at yearly intervals thereafter, if it is considered safe to do so on public protection grounds.

The Prison Service, working according to its Statement of Purpose, Vision, Goals and Values, and in partnership with the Probation Service, seeks to work positively and constructively with those doing life. It does so in a number of ways:

By keeping them in custody and ensuring the safety and protection of the public.

By allocating them to prisons whose regimes best meet the needs of the individual.

By helping them to come to terms with their offence.

By assisting them to identify, address and modify their problem behaviour and attitudes.

By ensuring that their suitability for release is objectively assessed by staff in a range of settings.

In order to manage life-sentence and indeterminate-sentence prisoners, the following underlying principles are followed:

They are treated as a group whose special needs are recognised within the prison, though not necessarily by separation or special privileges.

They have a planned and structured career through the prison system and where appropriate, progress to conditions of lower security.

Their allocation to prison establishments is managed centrally.

A typical prisoner in this category will go through a number of stages of the sentence prior to release on licence. There is no fixed time-scale:

Remand Centre/Local Prison.
First stage – High Security/Category B.
Second stage – High Security/Category B/Category C.
Third stage – Category D/Open/Semi-open/Resettlement.

Against such a background lifers in prison seek to live their lives.

Ten years ago I met Julian in a lifer main centre. In his early twenties, he had recently been given his 'tariff' – the minimum time recommended by the trial judge, and confirmed by the Home Secretary, following an opinion on it from the Lord Chief Justice. It does not guarantee a release date, and where release does take place, it is usually three years after the expiry of the tariff. For Julian, the tariff was 25 years, and the impact on him was devastating: 'I know the wrong I've done, I acknowledge my guilt, but 28 years in places like this doesn't bear thinking about. I don't know if I can hack it.'

It is hard to imagine how he felt. His guilt and remorse were compounded by the length of his tariff – more than the number of years he had already lived. In his despair he could only see darkness. Had he the courage, he said, 'I'd have killed myself, but that would be too easy. I have to be punished for what I've done.'

During the years which followed Julian and I spent much time together, discussing his offence – what had led to it, why he might have done it – for even he seemed to lack an explanation. He worked in the Braille Unit, spending three years obtaining his City and Guilds qualification, as he prepared Braille material for school text-books, the *TV Times*, and anything else that was needed by those without sight. Such was his dedication to helping such people that he eventually purchased his own Braille machine in order to work in his cell at night. Every few months, with the permission of the Governor, I transported the tins of food he had purchased in the prison canteen, and stored under his bed, to a night-shelter for the homeless in Leeds.

Two small gestures, as he saw them, of giving something back to the community he had deprived of a life. Symbolic gifts of restitution and reconciliation to a community disinclined to accept, inclined only to retribution. Yet, those acts contained within them, as restitution does, some element of healing, unlike retribution, which only inflames hatred. Julian, however, refused any part in his healing, determined to punish himself. Belief in God could not be translated into personal reconciliation, forgiveness, love. There was to be no 'cheap grace' for him, and I sat with him, empty-handed, my Christian 'tool-kit' for repair and restoration useless.

Julian is still in a high-security jail. His progress through the stages outlined above is slow. But with at least another 18 years to do, there seems little urgency. I think he presents little risk to the public, but there are those I have met who have been inside for over 30 years who, I believe, are not ready for release, and may never reach that point.

Shane is one. Despite his years in 'the system', he seems to be stuck in a mental time-warp upon which offending-behaviour programmes have had little impact. He shows no sign of increased self-understanding, much anger, and an inability to cope with any form of rejection. He seems as likely to re-offend now as ten or twenty years ago. For some, life may have to mean life.

> The Lord is merciful and gracious, slow to anger and abounding in steadfast love. He will not always accuse, nor will he keep his anger for ever. He does not deal with us according to our sins, nor repay us for our iniquities.
>
> Psalm 103:8–10

God of life,
you are merciful and gracious;
slow to anger,
and of great goodness.
You offer us the possibility
and the potential
to be more than we are,
to respond to your promise
of love and forgiveness.
Touch us with your grace
that in our disillusion
we may hold to you.

We hold before you
those who are 'doing life',
that in them your presence
may be acknowledged.
We commend to your care

> *those who feel the stigma*
> *of being 'lifers', aware that*
> *they will always be 'on licence'*
> *and rarely free to be*
> *the person they would wish.*
>
> *As Jesus was stigmatised,*
> *but never deserted, so we ask*
> *that you will be with those*
> *for whom life is diminishing.*
> *As Jesus was transformed*
> *by your power into new life,*
> *so may the gift of life*
> *be available to all your people.*

Information

The main types of life sentence are:

A mandatory life sentence, which is the only sentence the courts can impose for an adult found guilty of murder.

A discretionary life sentence, which might be given for a serious sexual or violent offence, where there is no fixed time imposed by the law. Examples would be arson, rape and manslaughter. Such sentences are usually passed where it is not possible to determine at the time of the sentence whether the prisoner will be safe to release at the end of a determined time. It could also be used to highlight the seriousness of the offence.

An automatic life sentence, which, in the absence of exceptional circumstances, the courts must impose on anyone aged 18 and over who was convicted of a second serious violent or sexual offence. This sentence was effectively replaced in 2005 with the introduction of the Indeterminate Sentence of Imprisonment (or Detention) for Public Protection (IPP and DPP). An Indeterminate Sentence of IPP is imposed where the offender is over 18 years of age and is convicted of a serious specified (as in Schedule 15 of the Criminal Justice Act 2003) violent or sexual offence, and in the court's opinion, presents a significant risk of harm to the public.

The situation is slightly different for Young Offenders (those under the age of 21). Five possible sentences may be imposed:

Detention during Her Majesty's pleasure. In effect this is the equivalent to a mandatory life sentence and is the only possible sentence for a person convicted of murder who was over the age of 10 but under 18 at the time of the offence.

Detention for life, which is the equivalent of a discretionary life sentence. Such a sentence must be used for people over 10, but under 18, and convicted of offences other than murder for which a discretionary life sentence may be passed on a person over 21.

Custody for life, which is the sentence for a person aged 18 or over, but under 21 at the time of the offence, who is convicted of murder.

For a person over 18 but under 21 at the time of the offence, and who is convicted of any other offence for which a life sentence may be passed on an adult, the court shall, if it considers that a custodial sentence for life would be appropriate, sentence him or her to custody for life.

A sentence of Detention for Public Protection (DPP) is imposed for those under 18 convicted of a serious specified violent or sexual offence, who, in the court's opinion, pose a significant risk of harm to the public.

Calendars, diaries and
the word

'Give us one of them diaries, mate,' is a frequent request around the landings of the prison, and not just at the start of the year, but throughout. So too is the demand for calendars. Most of those who ask would never be seen in the chapel, where diaries and calendars are always available. And yet for many, the diaries which the chaplaincy makes available, courtesy of Day One Christian Book Publications, and the calendars, from the Trinitarian Bible Society, may be the only Christian reading material they will ever see, let alone request. For some, the material, with its Scripture text for each day of the year, is the means by which they begin to reflect on the Christian message, and there are stories told of lives being transformed through its use.

Whilst some people simply want something for nothing, and others want a diary 'that's just the right size for my pocket', there are those who have said that the words in the diaries or on the calendars have caused them to think again about some of the things Christianity is saying. A few have said they have reconsidered the direction of their lives. Terry spoke for some: 'Prison really tries to destroy your spirit. It's a bad place to be, man. There's not much good here, yet the diaries help you cope, like. Some of it's a bit soft, but some has meaning.' In this way the seed may be sown.

In 1978, the first year the diaries were introduced to prison, 150 were distributed in HMP Dartmoor. The current annual figure is 180,000.

The availability of calendars in many languages is also of great help and can bring joy to some of the foreign nationals detained in prisons in this country. Our Muslim colleagues, recognising a similar need amongst Muslim prisoners, have distributed calendars for some years, and the first Islamic diaries for prisoners were distributed in 2008 – 9000 were printed. The Buddhist prison chaplaincy organisation, Angulimala, also produces calendars for Buddhist prisoners.

... he sustains all things by his powerful word.

Hebrews 1:3b

I planted, Apollos watered, but God gave the growth.

1 Corinthians 3:6

Blessed Lord,
who caused all holy Scriptures to be written for our
*   learning:*
help us so to hear them,
to read, mark, learn, and inwardly digest them
that, through patience, and the comfort of your holy word,
we may embrace and for ever hold fast
the hope of everlasting life,
which you have given us in our Saviour Jesus Christ.

Common Worship, The Last Sunday after Trinity

First time ... only time?

A young man in his mid twenties, a professional person who had been born and educated in one of the Eastern European countries, his English was fluent and articulate. This was his only experience of prison, arising from a situation which reflected a complicated dispute concerning his ethnic origin. A situation, however, with which I could identify. Given my own roots in another country, I felt I could echo, 'There, but for the grace of God, go I.' Such situations do exist and this young man had been in one of them, and was paying the price.

A regular member of a congregation in the Orthodox tradition, he adapted with surprising ease to the informal and non-liturgical acts of worship which I led in the chapel adjacent to the wing where he was held. Services were attended by some adult prisoners, and some young offenders. I was able to get him a copy of the Bible in his native (Czech) language, thanks to one of the Bible Societies. He was grateful and our discussions continued over the weeks he was in prison. He was interested to hear about this book, and he offered to write something about the questions which arose from the incident and his subsequent imprisonment. He wrote:

If we are prepared to accept, for a moment, that the courses of our lives are predetermined, then we can give consideration to the expression, 'It was meant to happen,' as a way of explaining an obviously unjust term of imprisonment in one's life. It is right to say that throughout the centuries, mankind evolved accustomed to the existence of an all-powerful God to whom we attribute the control of our lives. Therefore, it is to God that people rightly turn in their darkest moments, echoing invariable questions: 'Why me?', 'What have I done to deserve this?'

There are no direct answers to this kind of question and

consequently people are often left in a state of self-analysis, particularly where someone is innocent. There is no satisfactory answer in prison and so this state exists on release.

In fact, this is the state I am in at the moment, as I approach the end of my sentence. Frustrating as it is, I haven't found a compelling reason why God has given me such an experience, such a terrible trial. I've been through so much over the past year.

Returning to the initial issue, if it was really meant to happen, then I'm left wondering why I was given this imprisonment. I'm a professionally educated and disciplined man, a worthy contributor to society. What was this unfortunate experience supposed to have taught me?

Imprisonment, without doubt, can be one of the worst living nightmares, and had it not been for my self-discipline, my ability to accept limitations, this whole experience would have become an even greater nightmare. This is how I am left contemplating. What am I supposed to have learnt from this trial? It was not until the final part of my sentence that I understood I was not to learn something, but it was to show me something. Imprisonment has shown me a side of human nature that otherwise would have been impossible to know in depth, first hand. I have also come to realise the importance of my girlfriend in my life, and the depth of our relationship has grown. But even so, on the eve of my release I am still wondering why I had to pay such a terrible price for revealing something that could have been made obvious in some other, less frustrating way?

And it is in considering these questions that I accept that God works in mysterious ways, and his ways are indeed, at times, incomprehensible. But in all, I tend to believe that every difficult and arduous trial given by God is for the better, that adversity may be in fact a blessing in disguise, and that God walks with us through life's storms, and that great gain can come through great loss.

In the end, it is the apostle Peter who clearly expresses my hope:

Now who will harm you if you are eager to do what is good? But even if you do suffer for doing what is right, you are blessed. Do not fear what they fear, and do not be intimidated ... For it is better to suffer for doing good, if suffering should be God's will, than to suffer for doing evil.

1 Peter 3:13–14, 17

Accept suffering and be redeemed by it.

Fyodor Dostoevsky

Lord God,
in our quest for answers
we often reveal more questions.
Help us live with uncertainty
in an uncertain world.
Enable us to discover
that which is good,
even in our suffering.
Surround us with the mystery
and joy of your love,
that at the end
all things may be understood
and all may be well.

Name-calling

The vans, or 'sweat-boxes', waiting to transport their charges to Courts throughout the region were lined up in the prison yard. Winter grime had made it easy for the graffiti writers: 'Monster transport' was written in large letters down one side. 'Criminal carrier' was one of the more repeatable adornments on the back.

Every so often, there are calls from some newspapers to 'name and shame' 15–17 year-olds who presently cannot be named, by law. John Braithwaite, an Australian criminologist, is one of the foremost proponents of this approach, which he calls 'reintegrative shaming'. He contends that punishment must shame the offender, and in so doing bring home the reality of the offence to that person. He acknowledges that to succeed, such shaming must be reintegrative, or it may become stigmatisation and thus, counter-productive.

Braithwaite argues it is possible to express disapproval through shaming within a relationship which is based on respect for the offender. It is shaming which focuses on the sin and not the sinner.

The danger is stigmatisation, and the frequent use of names such as 'monster', 'pervert', 'evil' and 'beast' by the media helps to create outcasts of some offenders. A few years ago, a 14-year-old delinquent who found safe refuge from the police in a ventilation system on a housing estate was soon being called 'Ratboy'. It was left to his mother to affirm who he was as a person when she declared, 'He's not a rat. He's my son.'

And within the prison the most obvious 'outcasts' are those people on Rule 45, particularly the sex-offenders – the 'nonces', as they are named by the others.

Such name-calling or shaming can certainly affect those on the receiving end, and the stigma attached can be incredibly hard for some to bear. In an environment where relationships are tenuous at best, there is often little attention paid to the whole person and to their potential to be more than just 'names'.

As a former Archbishop of Canterbury, William Temple, reminded us, 'The prisoner is never only a criminal and nothing else ... it is good to think more of what the man may become than of what he is ... to treat the character as what it may be is to treat it as what in actuality it is, for it is chiefly potentiality.' And Sr Helen Prejean, an American nun who ministered to inmates on death row, reminds us that 'prisoners are always more than the sum of their deeds.'

> The soldiers also mocked him, coming up and offering him sour wine, and saying, 'If you are the King of the Jews, save yourself!' There was also an inscription over him, 'This is the King of the Jews.'
>
> Luke 23:36–38

> *Lord Jesus,*
> *you were named, and mocked.*
> *Mary's son, transforming*
> *the stigma of death*
> *with dignity and self-respect*
> *rooted in faith.*
> *As you called for forgiveness*
> *for those who mocked you,*
> *grant to us that spirit.*
> *As we were named in baptism*
> *so may we enter into life*
> *and achieve our potential in you.*

Segregation

In the Segregation Unit, where a Chaplain visits every day to see all prisoners (as is required by the Prison Act), the Staff asked me: 'Do you want to see Smith?'

'Yes,' I replied, 'anyone and everyone.'

'He's a bit of a mess,' was the response.

As I was led to the 'strip cell', my heart-rate increased and my anxiety rose. The 'strip cell' (now referred to as 'special accommodation') is used as little as possible. It has a concrete bed, just inches off the floor, and a concrete stump with a wooden top, which is a seat. There is no window and nothing on which a prisoner might do himself an injury. The door opens outward, and as it did I saw the blood stains on the walls and the floor. Dried now, they seemed like enormous tears, the visible signs of this man's internal anguish.

I entered and crouched down on the floor beside the slightly raised concrete/wooden bed, displaying in this gesture my own vulnerability. He was writing, hesitantly and with a fraughtness I had often seen in him on the Main Wing. Quietly, I said 'Hello.'

'The voices have left me,' he said, 'but now I don't know how to cope with my thoughts.' He continued writing, a list of 35 causes of personal concern he could express at that moment.

The upper part of his body was naked, the canvas (untearable) sheet covering his lower body. The blood-stained bandages covered both wrists. The signs of other self-inflicted injuries continued to his elbows.

Two officers remained close by, sensitive to my need to communicate with this man by myself, but near enough to be aware of any change in him, or me. My safety was their concern.

He talked rapidly and in myriad directions. It was clear that we could only begin to engage when he returned to the Main

Wing. I encouraged him to do so, and a few hours later we met again and talked.

I left the cell, stepping over a grating which covered the drainage system which allowed the cell to be hosed out, power-cleaned, washing away the visible signs of inward pain.

> *Father,*
> *in the depths of anguish*
> *you are there.*
> *In the brokenness of our lives,*
> *you are there.*
> *In the torment we inflict on*
> *each other, you are there.*
> *No situation is beyond your presence.*
> *In our gestures, in our words,*
> *may we recognise you.*
> *In symbolic and simple action,*
> *may we find you.*

Worship

'It's a short step between heaven and hell,' said one prisoner in a group discussion. We had been talking about the place of the chapel in the lives of those who attended, and this comment referred to the fact that access to the chapel, in this prison, was directly from the twos landing, on a wing with about 200 people. The contrast between the noise, clamour and occasional violence of the wing, and the peace, relative comfort and prayerfulness of the chapel, was very striking.

The chapel is used for a number of different activities, all of them in keeping with its primary purpose – that of providing a place for worship. It is here that the worshipping Christian community of the prison gathers week by week as part of the offering of worship made by the whole Church.

The worship style is varied, depending on whether it is led by an Anglican, Methodist, Roman Catholic or Baptist member of the Team. Always, it seeks to 'connect' to the experience of those present in some way, especially through the intercessions.

In worship we try to give 'worth' to God, and to each other. Sometimes it happens more easily than others, and when it does, those moments of 'transcendence', when the ordinary and the mundane are transformed, become moments to be treasured, and in which God seems so active.

Clifford, shortly before his release, provided such a moment. He was an able reader of lessons and I asked him if he would lead the intercessions this particular Sunday. He did so, with background music provided by a cassette of hymns played on classical guitar. The track was 'Be still for the presence of the Lord'. Apart from this, and the sound of Clifford's voice, not a sound could be heard. Even those outside the chapel could not impinge on the created silence. When he had finished, people simply sat, in the presence of God.

Clifford, as a prisoner, spoke from the same 'place' as other members of the congregation that morning, and he started by affirming the worth of each before God. With his permission, I reproduce the 'core' of his prayers:

Father,
Help us to face and accept the reality of our present situations, whether we are here for days, for months, or even longer.

Help us to admit past mistakes and also the consequences of our actions, the damage to others.

Help us to take that further step – to find true repentance in our hearts, and help us to show this clearly and honestly: to ourselves, to the world, and, above all, to you.

Help us to achieve that honesty in ourselves which will give us the courage to take a new path – for the sake of our loved ones and for the sake of our relationship with you.

Help us within our present enclosed world to temper resentment and aggression and to show understanding and fellowship towards both our fellow inmates and towards staff.

Help us with the world outside – to show family and friends that we need their love, loyalty and support; that we receive this thankfully – and that we respond.

Help us to open ourselves fully to you, to accept that we need above all else your love and support – and to have faith that this will always be given – that the burden of being made in your image will be eased by that faith and by our knowledge of you.

May our present situation be used by you to sanctify us.

After the silence that followed these prayers, we started to prepare for communion. Despite the frustrations of making relevant worship in this place, where else could I have the privilege of standing with people who would be amongst those Christ invites to the banquet? That morning, the body and blood of Christ was shared with sex offenders, robbers, fraudsters, drug addicts, alcoholics, and a murderer. In these people

I meet Christ and share with him, and them, in the joyful task of the proclamation of God's love. During communion the organist played the tune 'St Botolph', and the words of Brian Wren's hymn, 'I come with joy', came to mind:

> I come with Christians far and near
> to find, as all are fed,
> man's true community of love
> in Christ's communion bread.[12]

A moment in worship can provide a glimpse into the mystery of salvation. Many years later, and following his release, I still hear from Clifford by letter. In his seventies, he continues to attend worship in his parish church, to read the lesson, and to lead the intercessions.

Young offenders

At any time, there are about 9500 people aged 18–20 in prison in England and Wales. Young offenders often have poor literacy and numeracy skills, with nearly 75 per cent having been excluded from school at some stage. Around 63 per cent are unemployed when arrested. Mental-health problems and drug and alcohol abuse are common. Young offender institutions, and juvenile establishments, have the highest assault rates of any prisons in England and Wales.

This group of people are often more demanding and difficult than any other in the prison system. They are frequently frustrating, verbally aggressive and requiring particular skills of ministry, as is illustrated in the following story by an experienced chaplain.

Michael was a bigot, or so he would have us believe. To him, Irish, Roman Catholic, male (him) equalled good. English, Protestant, female (me) equalled bad. It was in the light of this apparent bigotry that we built up a pretty solid relationship over a period of two years. He attended most of the chapel activities, so we saw each other at least twice a week and cheerfully hurled abuse at each other.

But Michael was an intelligent young man and the facade of bigotry he had built up hid a lot of pain. He had been orphaned as a child and he had been convicted of a particularly nasty crime that he had to keep secret from other prisoners if he were to survive in the system. I think there was only one occasion when, in a private interview for the purpose of a parole report, a little of the facade slipped and a hurt, sensitive young man was revealed.

In many ways I did nothing for Michael apart from always being there, listening if he had something to complain about, and giving back as good as I got when the banter was flying.

After he was released, I had a letter from him thanking me for my kindness. Kindness ...? I was only ever rude to him. In the envelope was a prayer. Apparently Michael's mother used to give a copy of the prayer to anyone she knew who was in trouble. When she died a friend carried the habit on for her, and so Michael himself eventually received a copy when he came into prison. The letter told me he thought his mother and her friend would approve of him giving his own copy to me.

It is a gift I treasure. I trust God goes with Michael and I continue to pray for him regularly.

> So let us not grow weary in doing what is right, for we will reap at harvest time, if we do not give up.
>
> Galatians 6:9

A prayer written by Michael's chaplain:

> *Heavenly Father,*
> *Help us to love others in the same constant way you love us,*
> *not seeking great results but remaining faithful.*
> *Thank you that we only have to sow the seed*
> *and that the growing is up to you.*

Juveniles

I saw him in one of the long, characterless corridors of the juvenile unit. Looking lost and forlorn, Timmy seemed too young to be in such an austere and intimidating place. At 15 years of age, it was not his first time in trouble, but it was the first time he had been remanded in custody. One of about 2440 15–17 year-olds in prison (and 256 12–15 year-olds in privately run secure training units), his vulnerability was apparent. Since 1990, 30 children have died in penal custody, most by self-inflicted death. In November 2007 a 15-year-old boy was found hanging from a bed-sheet tied to the window-bars in a single cell on normal location. He was serving a sentence of one month and fourteen days.

Timmy, not even old enough to legally leave school, found his new surroundings intimidating and difficult to cope with as he waited for trial. We sat in his cell as he recounted his story with such speed that the sentences seemed to be continuous, reflecting his nervousness and anxiety. His parents had divorced and his mother had formed another relationship. Unable to form a positive relationship with her new partner, Timmy spent increasing time on the streets, getting involved with joy-riding when he was 11 years old.

Repeated minor offending caused further alienation from his family and from his school environment. Experimentation with drugs led to reliance on them and, within a short time of his fourteenth birthday, he was heavily involved in theft in order to pay for his 'habit'. Eventually, when repeated cautions from the police had failed, and when he had stolen from his mother, Timmy was arrested and remanded in custody. Now he waited, in an environment not likely to do him any good, but very likely to cause him harm – mental, physical, emotional.

Whilst Timmy and others like him are held in prison

accommodation, they may face emotional trauma and physical or emotional abuse, with consequent psychological damage. Such a scenario does not bode well for the future of such young people.

> *Gracious God,*
> *'slow to anger and of great goodness',*
> *we express our frustrations*
> *at the inadequacies of 'systems'*
> *which fail to reflect the needs*
> *of your people.*
> *In a damaging world,*
> *unstable and confusing,*
> *we pray for the young*
> *held in prison,*
> *that damage may be limited;*
> *that meaning may be kindled,*
> *and self-worth fostered;*
> *that failure may be seen*
> *as a chance for a new start.*

Information

During 2006/7, 93,730 young people entered the youth justice system for the first time.

Christmas

It was Christmas Eve, and the tree was being removed from the Wing where it had been placed just a few days before, its fallen needles exposing its barrenness. Its removal was a symbol of the marginalisation of the Christmas story which seemed to reflect my mood, itself a mirror image of an institution ill at ease with the 'festive season'. It exposed, too, the difficulty I find in connecting the joy and hope of that story with the lives of those 'inside'.

Later, as Christian members of the Chaplaincy Team delivered a hand-addressed Christmas card to over 700 prisoners registered as Christian, or 'Nil', a few were thrown back at us. In such a gesture, the 'rejection' seemed curiously personal, a rejection of 'self' as much as of God.

Christmas is a difficult time for many in prison and for their families, and the sombre mood seems in stark contrast to the world outside. A colleague in another prison wrote to me a note which arrived on that same Christmas Eve:

> It [the previous Christmas] was depressing. It was as if the season of goodwill had passed us by. Some men were in tears while others made the best of it by writing letters home to mother, wife or girlfriend – or boyfriend. Others had no one to write home to, so they hid themselves away, knowing that this most painful time would soon be over. Indeed, on Christmas Day last year I found one guy wrapped up tight in a blanket – like an Egyptian mummy – on the bed in his cell. He told me that he was in hiding and was not prepared to come out until it was all over. This was his first Christmas inside and during the previous nine months his wife had left him, his father had died, as had his grandmother.

At home, I read in the *Church Times* some words by a former Primus of the Scottish Episcopal Church, the Most Revd Richard Holloway. He said there were times when 'hope is low, and I am visited by a clear sense that there is no meaning and no beyond.' I fully concurred with him. But he went on to speak of the mystery of faith, and of our need 'to look at him whose birth we celebrate.'

The next day, Christmas morning, I had led one service, and now started another in the Prison Health Centre Chapel. The congregation preferred not to sing carols. 'Too painful,' said one, and the others agreed. A Rastafarian, who later spoke about his experience of discrimination and oppression, requested the hymn, 'Hail to the Lord's Anointed'. A powerful hymn about the mystery of the Incarnation, its words provided the means of connecting the divine story of the birth of Jesus with those in Chapel:

> He comes to break oppression,
> To set the captives free.
>
> His name shall stand for ever,
> His changeless name of Love.
>
> James Montgomery (1771–1854)

May he defend the cause of the poor of the people,
give deliverance to the needy.
For he delivers the needy when they call,
the poor and those who have no helper.

Psalm 72:4, 12

> *Lord, before you*
> *we express our doubt,*
> *and our faith;*
> *our anxiety*
> *and our certainty;*
> *our quest for meaning*

threatening to overwhelm
our sense of your presence.
In your Son
we acknowledge
the mystery of faith,
the encouragement of hope,
and the joy of his birth
as 'God with us'.

Easter

The Easter acclamation rang through the Chapel: 'Alleluia! Christ is risen.' And the response from the prison congregation came back to me: 'He is risen indeed. Alleluia!'

On this morning the sun shone through the Chapel windows, its force obliterating the thick iron bars, thoughtfully designed in the shape of the Cross, to proclaim the freedom of the faith, or the constraints of Christianity? It hardly mattered. Bars in prison are not a thing for comment.

I faced a group of men who had decided to come to Chapel that Easter morn. As with congregations 'outside', their motives were mixed. When it came to the sermon, I used the following piece, written by a prisoner serving time for robbery. It struck a 'ripple of responsiveness', and a few people said afterwards, 'I could have written those words – that's how it is for me. I ain't religious, but it said a bit about where I'm at.'

Gerry, who wrote it, called it 'Thought at Easter'. I have added a Bible reference and a prayer.

I'm not the kind of person who is ever likely to go to church, except of course for the obligatory weddings and funerals. I've never been much of a Christian. I'm not a Hindu, a Buddhist, a Muslim or a Jew.

Religion tends to bore me. After all, religion is only something man invented to make him feel good – isn't it?

It's about that time of year that Woolworths are going crazy trying to sell Easter eggs. The kids are happy, two weeks off school, an abundance of chocolate, all in all Easter's generally a nice time.

This Easter I'm in prison. This Easter I haven't seen a single chocolate egg. I regard the Bank Holidays with indifference. Two more slow days in prison, that's all. This year, for the first time ever I've thought about the significance of Easter. We all know the story. Jesus died on a Cross, then he came back, and Matthew, Mark, Luke, John and the rest of the boys decided they'd better tell the world about it.

We can't actually deny the truth in it. It's all in the Dead Sea scrolls, and other old manuscripts that prove it. But what's so special about this Jesus? In 2000 years' time I expect Mother Teresa will have achieved cult status. People like Terry Waite will go down in history as good examples, for all men and women to follow. So why is Jesus so special? Why not Joan of Arc, or a host of other people who died for a cause? Tonight I read all about Easter in the Bible. The whole story, from the donkeys and the palm leaves to the Resurrection.

When you really do think about it, it's easy to see what Christians all get so excited about. Whether Jesus was the Son of God or not isn't a question that I can personally answer. What I can say for sure is that he was flesh and blood like me. Jesus was a mortal man. He knew what was coming, and understandably he was sad and frightened at the prospect of his death. He actually prayed to God the night before he died. He did not want to die, yet he left it in God's hands. He trusted God.

Jesus knew that his friend Peter was going to sell him down the river. He knew that on the day of his death, three times Peter would deny him before the cock crowed. But he accepted this – he never judged Peter, or anyone. On the day he died people had a chance to save Jesus from the Cross, but they all stood and allowed the crucifixion to carry on. Jesus was taunted and humiliated. He had a crown of thorns wedged onto his head, cutting deeply into his scalp. Then he was nailed to a cross. Imagine the pain – huge nails driven through his hands and feet. The Cross was stood up and it fell into place in a hole that had been dug for it.

Now, Jesus felt the pain you or I would feel if we were on a cross. At one point he actually uttered, 'O Lord, why have you forsaken me?' Jesus was a man who had suffered incredible cruelty and humiliation, and now, he was left hanging in the sun to die. Then, as he was on the Cross, he forgave everyone.

He forgave Peter for selling out, he forgave the actual soldiers who had drove the nails through his flesh. In all that pain, all he could feel was compassion for all the people who had taken his life. He died asking God to forgive humanity its sins.

When I stop to think about that, it blows me away. I'm in prison for breaking the laws of the land. Fine, I can accept that. But sometimes it saddens me that the world will never really forgive me. I'll always be a robber in the eyes of many people. But when I think of Jesus up on the Cross, I feel humbled. All of a sudden, the few years I have to spend here don't seem to matter that much. As I said earlier, I've never been religious, but I do want to be forgiven by someone. I'm sorry for the wrongs I've done. The Judge doesn't know how I feel, the Police really don't care, and the victims of my crime probably find little peace of mind in the fact that I'm sorry for what I've done.

But Jesus, up there on that Cross, forgave people like me. He doesn't judge me, he doesn't hate me. He knows my wrongs, yet he still loves me. This is the first Easter I'll be spending in jail. The first of a few. But it's also the first Easter that I've actually realised what it's all about.

> 'And we indeed have been condemned justly, for we are getting what we deserve for our deeds, but this man has done nothing wrong.' Then he said, 'Jesus, remember me when you come into your kingdom.'
>
> He replied, 'Truly I tell you, today you will be with me in Paradise.'
>
> Luke 23:41–43

Lord, the thief responded
to the presence of your Son.
Help us to know his presence with us
that we may be transformed.

Jesus, remember us when you come into your kingdom.
As the thief acknowledged his need,

help us to be honest about ours.
And in repentance help us to
confess our sin.

Jesus, remember us when you come into your kingdom.

In the glorious light of the Resurrection
enable us to amend our lives
and to live as your people,
assured of your love and forgiveness.

Jesus, remember us when you come into your kingdom.

SITUATIONS IN
PRISON LIFE

Betrayal

His was a new face at worship. A Rule 45 prisoner, he was segregated from other prisoners (except for others on Rule 45) at all times, except in Chapel. (This situation has now changed and segregation is constantly maintained.) We were few in number that morning and I took the decision to move the focus of the service from the main altar to an improvised one using the coffee table, with easy chairs in the round.

It was a Eucharist and as usual I tried to explain what was happening as we came to each part. We sat in a circle and he sat near to me. In such a situation I take some responsibility for the safety of such men, despite the presence of two officers. They too sat within the circle. Sitting in the round means no one is separate, but part of the body. Within it, all are accepted in a way that is not possible anywhere else in the prison.

As it happened, the reading took the form of meditation. I asked people to try to enter into the reading, to use their imagination to become one of the characters; to enter into the scripture to discover insight for themselves, to absorb the scene, to try to be there; to let the story generate personal ideas and make connections. The silence was acute as I improvised the reading around Matthew's account of the betrayal of Jesus.

Afterwards, the Rule 45 prisoner and I spoke. He was not sure why he had come. The previous night he had felt he must come to Chapel the next day. He thought the feeling would pass, but it did not and in the morning he asked to attend Chapel. He was glad he had taken the step.

'I have been betrayed, and have betrayed,' he said. 'It was incredible how relevant that Bible story was. I never thought of Jesus having been betrayed, but he was, and I know what it feels like. I see him in a new light – perhaps he was like me.'

He had connected the divine story with his own, and in the

process had begun to deal with an aspect of betrayal. Jesus, a powerful figure in his imagination, somewhat feared and distrusted, became a brother in the experience of betrayal. Unlike this man, Jesus never betrayed.

See, my betrayer is at hand.

Matthew 26:46b

Lord Jesus Christ,
in your betrayal
you knew pain.
In our betrayal of others
we ignore the pain
we cause.
Help us attend to your story,
that through it we may
connect it with our own,
that through it we may begin
the process of healing
that leads to reconciliation.

Children

Geoff, a cleaner on the threes landing, called me over to his cell door. With a smile on his face, he said, 'Bill, I saw the kids last week.' His joy was evident. 'The Social Worker brought them up. Not together – the five-year-old one day, and the seven-year-old the next.'

I was touched by his joy, saddened at the depth of his anguish. He had endured uncertainty in their months of separation and he frequently said, 'Will I ever be allowed to see them, just once?' Now, he had. 'It was great to see them,' he said. 'And I've written letters for them to read when they're 18, explaining everything.'

At this point I found it hard to hold back my tears, even though I lived with the knowledge of his offence. Geoff continued his story, finishing off by telling me how the children had each thrown their arms around him at the conclusion of their visit, and said, 'I love you, Daddy.'

Almost as an afterthought, he added, 'Those words will keep me going for years.' Many years – for he is serving a life sentence.

Geoff's memory of those two visits will connect him with his past and will help to sustain him in his future. This connection between past events and our present touches upon a mystery which is deeply rooted in biblical tradition.

The people of Israel, in remembering God's great acts of love and kindness, seem, somehow, to enter into the acts themselves. The act of 'remembrance' is then more than just looking back at past events. It becomes a way of bringing those events into the present – to be celebrated and affirmed. Central to the biblical tradition is that God's love for his people should always be remembered and acknowledged in the present, in us now.

Geoff's former wife had agreed to this one visit. Despite the legal rights of fathers to see their children, many do not, believing that a pursuit through the courts is not in the interest of the child. Increasingly, however, parents in prison have a number of innovative ways of trying to maintain ties with their children.

Estimates indicate that up to 160,000 children have a parent in prison. Some 7 per cent of school-age children will experience the imprisonment of a parent, with at least 18,000 children separated from their mother. The number of children affected in this way is around two and a half times the number of children in care, and over six times the number of children on the child-protection register. It also means that each year more children experience the imprisonment of a parent than experience the divorce of parents. Children of prisoners are three times more likely to develop mental-health problems compared to their peers, and are likely to experience higher rates of social disadvantage.

> But Jesus said, let the children come to me, do not stop them; for it is to such as these that the kingdom of heaven belongs.
>
> Matthew 19:14

Loving Father,
in your Son
we see your love for all people.
We pray for the children
of those in prison,
parted from a parent.
Help us to understand
their needs and anxieties
as they try to make sense
of separation and pain.
Surround them with your love.

Lord, your Son responded
to the needs of children,

and through them proclaimed
something of your Kingdom.
We hold before you
imprisoned parents.
Relieve the pain of
separation which is theirs,
the joy which they have missed
and the sadness they cannot share.

Information

For more information go to www.prisonersfamilies.org.uk

Forgiveness

John was 23. Three years earlier he had been diagnosed as being HIV positive. The woman he lived with had been a prostitute and an intravenous drug user, but she had never told him about her past.

Returning home one day, he was told she was in a local hospital. When he got there and explained who he was, he was asked, 'Do you know she has Aids?' Devastated by this revelation, he watched and waited for her to die. Within a few short months, she was gone. She was 26. Carrying with him a profound anxiety about his own health, he was eventually persuaded to go for a test. It confirmed what he felt he already knew – he was HIV positive. She had infected him.

Three years have passed and his immune system functions at about half the 'normal' level. Since returning to prison, he has returned to faith; a faith which came about through the care shown him by a Christian family at the end of his previous sentence. Nothing dramatic had taken place for him, no 'Damascus road' experience; just the conscious building on the care shown to him, and attention to the suffering of Christ. 'In his suffering,' he told me, 'I see something of my own.'

John went on to explain how he felt about the forgiveness which Christ expressed towards those who caused his suffering. As a result of his faith, he said he had forgiven the woman who had infected him. He had watched her die, been with her, and when she had said 'Sorry,' he had forgiven her. Three years on, that sense of forgiveness was uppermost in his mind.

As so often in prison, I was left with a question, to which I could not provide an answer. A question arising from his capacity to forgive, borne out of love. I wondered if I could ever have a similar capacity.

Father, forgive them; for they do not know not what they
are doing.

Luke 23:34

> *God of forgiveness,*
> *help us forgive.*
> *God of forgiveness,*
> *help us know forgiveness.*
> *God of forgiveness,*
> *help us know*
> *peace in forgiveness.*
> *God of forgiveness,*
> *help us know*
> *love in forgiveness.* ·
> *God of forgiveness,*
> *help us know you*
> *in forgiveness.*
>
> *Lord, it is difficult to forgive,*
> *to know what it really means*
> *to offer it, to accept it.*
> *Yet you never give up on us*
> *and always accept us.*

Listening

Trevor was typical of many people in prison. He wanted someone to listen to him, to take him seriously, to acknowledge who he was, and to accept him 'warts and all'.

He took every opportunity to speak to me, rarely giving me much opportunity to respond to his endless flow of words. It took much attentiveness to discern what might have been behind some of what he said; it took time and patience to help him express some of the thoughts which lay deeply buried within his mind.

So many of those in prison have such harrowing stories to tell that the responsibilities of those involved in active listening are great. At times it requires enormous effort, perseverance and patience. Sometimes I think we listen with only one ear – we only half listen, too often presuming that we know what the other person is likely to say. And the assumption that we have to say something in response is an affliction which needs to be resisted (particularly by the clergy).

All too often, Trevor left what he really wanted to say to the time when our conversations were coming to a close. One is tempted to ignore what is being said at that moment, particularly if the pressure on time is great, as so often it is.

Dietrich Bonhoeffer, in his book *Life Together*,[13] is scathing about the ability of some Christians to fully enter into the 'Ministry of Listening', saying they are too busy talking when they should be listening. He goes on to say:

> One who cannot listen long and patiently will presently be talking beside the point and be never really speaking to others, albeit he be not conscious of it. Anyone who thinks that his time is too valuable to spend keeping quiet

will eventually have no time for God and his brother, but only for himself and his own follies.

For those who minister in prison, where there are so many demands, so much noise, so many things to be attended to, this is a salutary reminder, and in the Bible the verb 'listen' is used more frequently than the verb 'speak'. Bonhoeffer concludes his section on listening with the words, 'We should listen with the ears of God that we may speak the Word of God.'

If one gives answer before hearing, it is folly and shame.
Proverbs 18:13

Lord God,
you are more willing to listen
than we are to hear.

As we seek to listen
to those with whom we speak,
help us to acknowledge
the privilege and service
to which you have called us;
to respond to that trust.

In the clamour of our lives
we confess our fear of silence.
In our need to speak
we fail to hear the thoughts
of others;
fail to hear your presence.

Give us the gift of 'the ears of God,
that we may speak the Word of God.'

Relationships

Every new prisoner on remand, convicted or sentenced, is required, under the Prison Act 1952, to be seen by the Chaplain, or as happens in practice now, a member of the Chaplaincy Team. During the interview it is rare for a prisoner to claim to have no family or friends, no significant relationship.

Yet frequently, the relationships which do exist, within or without the prison, are damaged, tenuous, unpredictable, and there is a high rate of break-up between prisoners and their partners, and separation from their children and home community. There is bullying, assaults on staff and on other prisoners, self-harm and suicide. Increased numbers of people in prison can also affect the quality of relationships as staff have to deal with more people, with less time available to care for those in need. It may also mean some prisoners being moved from one part of the country to another, often at short notice, and with no regard for the impact on their relationships.

An additional and complicating factor relates to the number of people held on remand who should be in alternative custody – for example, in the care of the National Health Service, or a Secure Unit, because of their mental state. Being remanded in prison can lead to increased despair and anxiety for those people, and so to a worsening of their condition. For those staff who care for them, there is a feeling that they are ill equipped to provide appropriate support.

At the very heart of Christianity lies an understanding of the character of God which is based on the concept of relationships. It is exemplified in Andrej Rublev's Icon, *The Hospitality of Abraham*, in which three people, three angels, sit around a table. Representing the Trinity, they are three persons in relationship – Father, Son and Holy Spirit. The deep significance of this view of the Holy Trinity is well expressed in a Report by what was the British Council of Churches, *The Forgotten Trinity*: 'if God is essentially relational, then all being shares in relation. There is … a relational content built into the notion of being. To be is to exist in relation to other beings.'

Relationships between prisoners and their families, between prisoners and staff, prisoners and prisoners, staff and staff, are a crucial element in creating peaceful, co-operative and positive regimes in prison. Whilst the Prison Service recognises the importance of positive relationships between prisoners and their families, many are separated by considerable distance, often making visits very difficult. Accommodation pressures mean that on average men are held 50 miles, and women 55 miles, from their home or committal court address. Some 12,000 prisoners are held over 100 miles away. Increasing pressure on available accommodation in many prisons means this situation is likely to continue for the foreseeable future.

> Then the Lord God said, 'It is not good that the man should be alone; I will make him a helper as his partner.'
> Genesis 2:18

God of love,
in the Trinity
we see relationships
as they might be.
Individuals, but
sharing in common.
Separate, but united.

Forgive our lack
of love and respect
for each other,
our ability to disregard
our commonality
in pursuit of our individuality.

Help us affirm our relationships,
that, together, we may be nurtured.

Information

Almost 20 per cent of those remanded in custody are acquitted. Only about half of all remanded prisoners go on to receive a custodial sentence. As many as 75 per cent of male remand prisoners suffer from a personality disorder. One in ten have a functional psychosis, and more than half experience depression. Research has shown that 9 per cent of remand prisoners require immediate transfer to the National Health Service. (Information from www.prisonreformtrust.org.uk)

Remembrance

The daily 'reception' list of those who had arrived in the prison the previous evening was on my desk. I saw Ben's name, location, age, racial origin, number and religion. Jewish. In conversation he explained his background, but said he did not want to see the Orthodox Rabbi. I undertook to try to find a Rabbi from the Progressive or Liberal tradition.

In the meantime I gave him copies of the Jewish Daily Prayer Book, the Haftorahs and Pentateuch, and the Tanakh. Over the following weeks he spoke with me frequently. Never at great length but always in depth. He asked to become the Chapel Orderly when the post became vacant. Essentially a cleaning job, it is, nonetheless, a sensitive position.

Ben was seen by a Progressive Rabbi. In our talks and in discussion groups his interest in his faith tradition began to develop. He began to get in touch with his memories of childhood and Jewish traditions.

The memories which we have, within or without prison, play a central and crucial role in our sense of being, in our joy and in our pain. The feelings which we possess of grief and satisfaction do not depend only on the events, but on our memory of those events.

Ben began to explore those memories, to 'remember' his past, his tradition. As he did so, he began to connect his own story to that of his Jewish forebears. In remembering, he began to explore the tension between his past and his future, and through it he began to rediscover his identity and find a new meaning for his life.

We need to pay attention to the memories which are presented to us, for they have the power to change hearts. We sometimes have the privilege of helping people explore their memories, sometimes the joy of seeing them healed.

Then when you call upon me and come and pray to me,
I will hear you. When you search for me, you will find
me; if you seek me with all your heart.

Jeremiah 29:12–13

Remember the days of old, consider the years long past.

Deuteronomy 32:7

> *God of Israel,*
> *teach us to remember*
> *our past with gratitude.*
> *Enable us to remember*
> *your goodness and your love,*
> *that we may be your people now.*
> *We give you thanks*
> *for the gift of memory,*
> *for its part in shaping us*
> *and making us who we are.*

Vulnerability

A colleague said to me, 'What can I do when I'm in the Segregation Unit? I feel helpless, at a loss to know what to offer.' I responded by acknowledging my own difficulty in such situations, but believed in the concept of what sometimes seems to be 'useless presence' – a way of being with people, not of doing. Later, she wrote of one such experience, and each of us has added a prayer.

I sat very still and listened as the story unfolded. It began slowly, very slowly at first. It took time to tell because it had never dared to be told before. Well, how do you begin to share the pain and misery of a life systematically destroyed? Where do you start when all your childhood memories run red with blood, black with fear, and blue with coldness and brutality, the agony as vivid today as it was all those years ago? Who do you trust with that deep, open wound that is your life, and what will be the price you pay, if, having finally trusted someone, they let you down?

Suppressing an urge to move, I remained still, waited as the tears were wept, and the rage was expressed; staying as open and vulnerable as I could, risking as much as the story-teller. As calmness descended and the tears began to dry, Frazer asked, 'How did you do that? How did you help me to cry? How was that possible?'

How? It's simple, and difficult. There is only one real way into the pain of another. It involves risk to self, no doubt, but that is the price which has to be paid. Vulnerability is the key that opens the door of vulnerability. Nothing less will do. It is all that can be offered that is of any value, that is authentic. Vulnerability alone speaks to vulnerability. As it is offered, so is it recognised and welcomed, like a friend, like a soul-mate.

In the harsh world of prison there is little room for any show of what might be seen as weakness. So any vulnerability is screened from prying eyes. The need, however, to express the pain, the anger, the fear and the frustration remains. The chaplain has no need to collude with the macho image of the prison system, for the model for all Christian ministry is that of Christ himself, the epitome of vulnerability, hanging high on a cross, arms open wide. His refusal to defend his dignity, to protect his name, to save his life, resulted in his death, but that ultimate expression of humanity has touched the lives of millions for nearly 2000 years.

Is it too much to ask to be listened to by a fellow human being, to be treated with respect, to be given the opportunity to tell it how it was, without fear of the broken, shattered dreams being trampled into the ground all over again? To be vulnerable is to be human, but to share that, is to be Christ-like.

> ... a broken and contrite heart, O God, you will not despise.
>
> Psalm 51:17

Loving God,
we come to you
just as we are,
vulnerable and afraid.
We reach out to you
in trust and faith,
praying that in you
we will find peace,
acceptance and encouragement,
through Jesus the Lord.

Lord, in your Son
we see the cost of being vulnerable
to the expectations of others,
of being open to their pain
and vulnerability.

*As we encounter
those whose lives are broken,
help us confront our brokenness
to commend it to your
healing and transforming power.*

Mental illness

An inward and involuntary groan was my reaction to seeing Peter again. It was only a matter of weeks since he had been discharged, and now he had returned. Peter is just one of over 70 per cent of sentenced prisoners (male and female) who suffer from two or more mental-health disorders. He also has a dependency on alcohol, and he is one of a significant number of people who constantly come and go to and from prison, caught in a seemingly unending cycle of offending, arrest and trial, followed by institutional detention or care – a process sometimes referred to as the 'revolving door' syndrome.

In a women's prison, with nearly 400 prisoners, I sat with members of the chaplaincy team who described themselves as being 'overwhelmed' by the needs of women with mental-health issues. One chaplain, a trained counsellor, has a full-time case-load of people referred to her from all parts of the prison as she responds to those who have complex and long-standing mental-health issues.

As with Peter, all too often these needs are linked to substance misuse, and range from acute psychosis, through personality disorder, to high levels of anxiety and depression. These needs are, in turn, as the Chief Inspector of Prisons has highlighted, only part of a 'more complex picture of multiple disadvantage and social exclusion, which may fall through the net of community health, social care, housing, and drug agencies.' The Chief Inspector also said, 'prison has become, to far too large an extent, the default setting for those with a wide range of mental and emotional disorders.'

Martin Narey, a former Director General of the Prison Service, writing in 2002, said: 'Since the late 1980s, the proportion of the prison population who show signs of mental illness has risen seven-fold. For them, care in the community has become care in custody.' With almost 83,000 people in prison, some estimates say as many as 5000 are too ill to be held there.

In an extraordinary series of debates in every branch of the Women's Institute in England and Wales, and following further debate at their national conference, a vote was passed by 6205 in favour to 173 against. The motion was: 'In view of the adverse effect on families of the imprisonment of people with severe mental health problems, this resolution urges HM Government to provide treatment and therapy in a more appropriate and secure residential environment.' The motion came about because of the determination of a mother whose son had committed suicide in prison. A young man doing a doctorate in physics, he had been diagnosed with schizophrenia, and had ended up in prison.

Some staff in prison feel ill equipped to provide the sort of care which people such as Peter, and so many like him, are entitled to receive. As a consequence, staff anxiety may be heightened because of an awareness of the increased vulnerability of such people, producing a sense of helplessness mixed with hopelessness. The care of those with mental illness, as the Chief Inspector has acknowledged, must involve care and support from the full range of staff in prisons, and not just mental-health professionals. It requires a holistic approach, based on the concept of a 'healthy' prison, where prisoners are safe, treated with respect, able to engage in purposeful activity, and are prepared for release. Chaplaincy HQ is working with the Department of Health to provide training on the identification of those with mental illness, and how to respond to them. Over 9000 staff in prisons have already received similar training.

> Moved with pity, Jesus stretched out his hand and touched him …
>
> Mark 1:41

> Thou hast made us for Thyself, and our hearts are restless till they find their rest in Thee.
>
> St Augustine, *Confessions*

God of wholeness,
your Son encountered
the disturbed in mind
and body; in acceptance
he showed your love
and compassion.
In your love, be
present in the lives
of those who suffer
anguish of mind,
and in those who
offer them care.
Be present in their skills,
that they might foster
wholeness.

Information

See the mental health of prisoners thematic (2007) at www.inspectorates.homeoffice.gov.uk
For further information see Social Exclusion Unit (2002), *Reducing re-offending by ex-prisoners.*

Self-harm

Ian had lacerations from his wrist to his elbow, on each arm. When I saw him he had just cut both his cheeks. This latest attempt at self-harm was just one of over 22,000 such incidents recorded in prisons in England and Wales in one year. In 2006, women prisoners accounted for almost 50 per cent of self-harm incidents, despite being only 6 per cent of the prison population.

Self-harm is primarily a means by which people cope with the distress and despair in their lives, but sometimes people who self-harm go on to end their own lives.

Some people have seen such incidents of self-harm as being an attempt at manipulation. It is more likely to be because the person is trying to communicate a problem which is beyond their control at that time. Some are in despair about what they perceive as an intolerable position which crucially highlights their lack of self-esteem, their limited control over events, and their inability to convey to others their deep distress.

Some describe the feeling of intense relief which they experience once they have committed the act. It is thought-provoking, and disturbing, to consider that the letting of one's 'life-blood' may be the only way of finding relief, or drawing attention to a real problem.

As I sat with Ian, listening intently to all he told me, I was aware of my inability to carry such a load. He was the second person to speak to me in such a way within an hour. It was a Sunday. I had already taken two services and it was only just midday.

What could I offer to this man? How could I help him? How could I respond to his needs?

The reading at one of the services had been from James: 'be quick to listen, slow to speak ...' (1:19). Was that enough, I wondered?

Frank Lake, one of the founders of the clinical theology movement, quotes the novelist Taylor Caldwell (*The Man Who Listens*): 'Man's real need, his most terrible need, is for someone to listen to him, not as a "patient" but as a human soul.' We could replace 'patient' with 'prisoner'.[14]

Ian had a learning disability, and had been fostered from the age of two. He was now approaching his twentieth birthday, and lived in a group home under the policy of 'Care in the Community'. He was desperate, frustrated, angry with himself, and finding it hard to articulate his thoughts. I listened, finding it equally hard. Despite hearing it all from others many times before, it still pains me anew when I am faced with people like Ian: people who have never had any real chance, who have known little love, received little care; whose lack of self-esteem, self-worth and self-understanding cries out through their words and actions.

'Big boys don't cry,' it is said. Ian did. And I, inwardly.

Lake's words filled my mind and I fought to concentrate on Ian's words, constantly 'sifting' them to try to understand what he was saying, to patch together a mosaic of sadness, to respond positively, but realistically.

> You must understand this, my beloved: let everyone be quick to listen, slow to speak, slow to anger.
>
> James 1:19

Lord God,
in their trauma
they scar themselves.
In doing so
they scar your image;
for we are created
in like form.
Created for life,
they see only the negative,
the pain from
which they have come

and to which, so often,
they return.

Help us break the cycle
of destructiveness,
to give worth to those
who feel worthless,
control to those
without control,
hope to those
without hope,
that as with Christ,
you may heal the scars
which afflict us all.

Thoughts of suicide

After the morning service I deliberately sat next to one of the 'new faces' over coffee. At that time we had three services each Sunday, in three chapels located in different parts of the prison. Had all three congregations been together, they would have made up one good-sized group. As it was, there were ten men at this communion service and I was able to give Alan some time. He had not been to church for many years and certainly not in the three months he had so far been in prison. 'I'm not very religious,' he said. 'I don't go to church very often.' Not an unusual line for ministers to hear, either in prison, or outside.

As we talked, he began to reveal a little more about himself. I already knew he was a Rule 45 prisoner, segregated because of the nature of his alleged offence. Not that I was aware of the details of his alleged crime, but I knew he came from the Wing which housed such men. I also knew he was on remand. Prison seems to make some prisoners get to the heart of what they want to say very quickly, and Alan was soon telling me of a religious experience which he had in his cell.

As soon as such conversations start to go in this sort of direction, my instinct is to be cautious. On this occasion I was intrigued by what I heard.

Alan recounted some of his feelings during his first few days in the prison some 12 weeks before. He had never been inside and had not expected he would be. In his cell he experienced powerful and recurring urges to commit suicide over a number of days. He spoke of these feelings to no one. One night he decided he had had enough; he was going to kill himself. Some memory from his childhood made him reach for the Gideon Bible. Randomly he opened it and read the first words he saw on the page:

The snares of death encompassed me;
the pangs of Sheol laid hold on me;
I suffered distress and anguish.
Then I called on the name of the Lord:
'O Lord, I pray, save my life!'
Gracious is the Lord, and righteous;
our God is merciful.
The Lord protects the simple;
when I was brought low he saved me.

Psalm 116:3–6

At the conclusion of verse 6 he read no further. Nor did he try to commit suicide. The thoughts remained with him for some time, but he knew he could not go through with the action. He attributed his change of mind to God speaking through the words of the Psalm. Now, weeks later, he was ready to encounter God in worship, to speak about what he felt to be God's action in his life.

Subsequently, Alan was convicted of his offence. Many months later, he is still convicted about God's part in his being alive.

Faithful God,
we give you thanks that
you rescue us from our faithlessness.
Help us to hear your voice in Scripture
and in the experience of those we meet.
We give you thanks for
the word which changes lives,
for the word which affirms
and gives meaning.
Enable us to respond
to your word as you
respond to our prayers.

Information
The Gideons supply thousands of Bibles and New Testament &
Psalms to prisons. For more about their work, see the story,
'The word across the prison world' (p. 215).

Suicide

During 2007, there were 92 self-inflicted deaths in prisons in England and Wales, an increase of 37 per cent on the previous year. This followed successive years in which there were significant reductions. The numbers, thankfully, began to fall again early in 2008, but remain worryingly high. Eight women and seven people under 21 were included in the 2007 numbers for self-inflicted deaths. The youngest was 15 years of age. Of those who died, 41 were on remand, and 23 were foreign nationals. On any one day there are over 1500 people assessed as being at particular risk.

Frances Crook, Director of the Howard League for Penal Reform, has said:

> A leap of 37 per cent in the annual prison suicide rate is the human cost of the prisons crisis. The prison service has taken great strides in suicide prevention in recent years but it is all for naught when the system is on its knees with record overcrowding. Staff and resources are strained to the limit coping with an ever-swelling prison population rife with mental health problems, drug and alcohol addiction and histories of neglect and abuse. Prison is where we seek to sweep away social problems, blithely unaware of the fact that we are simply compounding the problems we seek to avoid.

Now, as Chaplain General, one of the things I seek to do (or one of my colleagues does it) is to contact every chaplaincy in a prison where there has been a suicide, to offer support, practical and prayerful.

When I was a chaplain in Norwich Prison, more than one of the 'statistics' was known to me. Rati was 26 years of age and was born in Sri Lanka. Convicted and sentenced to three years, he had served two and had come to the end of his time in prison. Now, he was being detained pending the outcome of discussions with the Immigration Service, who had advised him of the likelihood of deportation. He spoke good English and on a few occasions he came to chapel, even though he was a Hindu. Whilst I was on leave, he took his own life.

Those of us who knew him, just a little, felt we had let him down, had not recognised his isolation and his deep fear of deportation. The sense of loss was acute amongst the landing-staff concerned, particularly the officer who had shared a 'good-night' with him as he locked Rati in his cell, only to find he had taken his own life. Rank and position faded as staff shared a common sense of grief. No relatives could be traced, despite extensive efforts by many people.

With no Hindu chaplain at the time, but with the help of some members of the small local Hindu community, I arranged for his cremation. With five members of that community I sat in the crematorium chapel and thought of our failure. Rati, surrounded by people, had died alone, 'a stranger in a foreign land'.

Despite the 'coherent multi-disciplinary suicide prevention strategy' employed by the Prison Service, including ACCT (Assessment, Care in Custody, Teamwork), a care-planning system for at-risk prisoners, despite the then increase of male suicide in the wider community, despite the 'high risk' of many in prison, despite the success of the Prison Service in preventing so many from taking their own life, despite my knowledge that not all suicides are preventable – I felt I had let Rati down.

I was reminded of some words of John Donne: 'No man is an island ... any man's death diminishes me, because I am involved in mankind.' With others, I share deeply, and ashamedly, in that diminution.

How could we sing the Lord's song in a foreign land?

Psalm 137:4

Lord of life,
look with mercy and compassion
on those, who, in despair,
have taken their own lives.
In your love, may they
find light, peace,
and life eternal.

Information

The ACCT care-planning procedure is part of the way in which concerns about a prisoner are managed. It includes input from the prisoner so he/she has a part in his/her self-management, which can be empowering.

For more information visit www.justice.gov.uk

See also 'Thoughts of suicide' (p. 142), 'Samaritans and Listeners' (p. 147) and 'Self-harm' (p. 139) in this book.

Samaritans and Listeners

Listeners are prisoner volunteers who are selected, trained and supported by local Samaritan branches. There were, in February 2008, 143 Listener schemes operating in 169 prisons in England, Ireland and Wales, and around 1200 active Listeners in those prisons. Listeners receive regular support through direct contact with Samaritans during weekly support meetings in the prison, and they are also able to phone Samaritans at any time to off-load after a difficult contact.

Listeners are trained in basic listening skills and suicide awareness, based on standard Samaritans training, adapted for use in the prison setting. They also have regular access to their trainers, and to those Samaritans responsible for supporting them and helping them to work through difficulties or feelings which they experience in the course of this vital work, which is a unique form of prisoners helping each other in custody.

The Samaritan movement, founded in 1953, usually works in prison through the multi-disciplinary Safer Custody Team to offer confidential and emotional support to prisoners, and where necessary, to staff. The policy of confidentiality for Listeners is exactly the same as it is for Samaritans volunteers, and is vital for encouraging prisoners considering suicide to use the service. There are some very specific exceptions to this – for example, a confidence that would contravene the Terrorism Act 2000, or if the prisoner is attempting to take his or her own life.

Listener schemes have proved to be a valuable resource, amongst others, in helping prisoners who are anxious, in despair, or potentially suicidal. Such a sharing of responsibility, between staff, Listeners and outside agencies, for vulnerable individuals is a reflection of a relational approach to caring in a complex environment.

'Which of these three do you think was a neighbour to
the man who fell into the hands of the robbers?'

He said, 'The one who showed him mercy.'

Jesus said to him, 'Go and do likewise.'

Luke 10:36–37

God of mercy and compassion,
we commend to you the work of
Samaritans and Listeners;
foster their ability to show
mercy and to hear the stories
of those who are anxious,
depressed or suicidal,
to accept them, and in so doing
to help the healing of hearts and minds.
May their ministry reflect
your purposes.

Innocent

Andrew and I first met when he had been incarcerated for 14 and a half years. Immensely shy, this large and amiable man made a deep initial impression on me, and on my Roman Catholic colleague. He had recounted his story to each of us and had given us permission to reflect together on his situation. He had spent a number of years in a special hospital for the criminally insane, and had now returned to prison as new evidence about his case began to emerge.

Many protest they are innocent of the crime for which they have been imprisoned. A few have convinced me, usually after a long period of time has elapsed. Andrew was different. He seemed to exude innocence and my colleague and I quickly formed an opinion that he was one of the few. Yet, questions came to mind. How could an innocent person have spent 14 and a half years in prison? Surely, all the evidence had been unequivocal? And believing him, how could we make known our belief in his innocence?

Andrew talked quietly, but with frightening clarity, about his conviction, and his initial rage, bewilderment and indignation at losing his freedom for something he had not done. His continued denial of guilt had probably contributed to his still being in prison, for the system does not cope easily with such dissent. Over those long years he seemed to have turned his feelings inward, on himself, but his anxiety rarely surfaced. His presence disturbed us both, as we colluded in his continued imprisonment, helpless though we were to do otherwise.

Within 18 months he was freed, declared to have been physically incapable of committing the crime for which he had served 16 years in prison.

On television, I watched this man take his first, faltering steps of freedom, and my tears welled up. There were to be more tears. Two years later, he died, his story of innocence vindicated. Fourteen years later, someone else was convicted for the murder Andrew had not committed.

And in their mouth no lie was found; they are blameless.
Revelation 14:5

Father God,
whose innocent Son
suffered death on the Cross,
we pray for those
who are imprisoned
though they have done
no wrong.
Enable us to sit
where they sit;
to support their plea
and to help them rise
with Christ, in joyful hope.

'Ghosting'

'Be careful of that one, Chaplain', said the officer in the Segregation Unit. 'He's been no bother, yet, but he has been in other places.'

Ever mindful of such warnings, I approached Stan with care as he walked around the small exercise yard, a space not much bigger than that afforded to a 'big cat', and just as difficult to escape from. Having introduced myself, I walked by his side. Despite the confines of such places, there is theological significance in 'walking with', in a ministry of presence. The summer sun shone on the fraction of the exercise yard it was able to penetrate. Our conversation was not much more enlightened, at least initially.

Stan told me a little of his story. He had been in prison for just over ten years, for a crime, he claimed, he did not commit. A claim I hear frequently, it is occasionally true.

'What has brought you to this prison?', I asked.

'I've been ghosted, again,' he replied.

'Ghosted' is the term used by some Category A prisoners to describe the process which sometimes means they are moved without notice, from one prison to another, usually for reasons of security or good order. Stan had been in a number of different prisons since the start of the year. As if reciting a litany, he named each one for me, with acerbic comments where appropriate.

Over the days that followed, Stan told me much about himself, about the prison system on which he is an expert, and about the powerful, negative effects his 'moves' had on his family, his friends, and himself. Such prisoners are never told exactly when they will be moving, and on more than one occasion Stan's visitors arrived at the prison where he was being held, only to find he had been moved. Personal possessions are minimal because of the movement. Letters take time to 'catch up' with the prisoner. The stress imposed by uncertainty and new surroundings is considerable.

The philosopher, John Locke, said that human beings are the property of God and, using this concept as his base, he developed the doctrine of natural human rights. It is because we are God's 'property', God's people, that we have rights which should protect us from abuse or mistreatment by another, be it an individual or an institution. Justice is not always easy to define, but we might do well to think first about injustice.

> Now, let the fear of the Lord be upon you; take care what you do, for there is no perversion of justice with the Lord our God …
>
> 2 Chronicles 19:7

> While they were talking and discussing, Jesus himself came near and went with them.
>
> Luke 24:15

God of justice,
open our eyes
to the injustice we create
in pursuit of order.
Enable us to respect
the rights of your people,
to seek for their good,
to show them
the way of peace,
which is yours.

We pray for prison staff
entrusted with the duty of care
for such people, who are not
always easy to deal with,
or easily liked.
May duty be tempered
with compassion.

Paedophiles

There are over 7000 convicted sex-offenders in prison.

The subject of paedophilia is highly emotive and confusion over definitions often exists. A paedophile is a man (very occasionally, a woman) with a fixed interest in pre-pubescent children. Most of those convicted of sexual offences against children do not in fact fit this description. Contrary to some people's opinion, they are not 'monsters' and easily identifiable in the community. If they were, they would not get close to children. But they are people who believe that children can give their consent to sexual activity. Indeed, some believe that the children with whom they are involved have, somehow, 'encouraged' them. They are capable of identifying, encouraging and seducing a child, often rationalising their thought process by convincing themselves that the child is enjoying what is happening. If they have been abused themselves as children (and not all who are abused become abusers), they may convince themselves that they enjoyed such activity and that they gave their consent, and that the child with whom they are involved thinks in the same way. They are often people who have been emotionally isolated and have difficulty in coping with emotional stress; they tend to have low self-esteem and are poor at appreciating how others might be feeling.

Whilst they cling to the sort of belief system that enables them to abuse, they find that legitimisation is given to their acts by support groups in this country and abroad. With magazines and easily available internet material endorsing such thought processes, some of these people feel they have not done wrong.

One man I knew who had regular sexual intercourse with his young daughter justified his actions to me by saying, 'It was an act of love, and my wife encouraged it to happen.' Such distortion and minimisation can be problematic, and since 1992 treatment has been available to sexual offenders in prison in England and Wales. To date, some 7600 have taken part, on a voluntary basis. The programmes are based on a form of treatment called 'cognitive behavioural therapy', and are aimed at altering the way in which men think about the images which arouse them and lead to illegal sexual acts. The programmes also help offenders to gain some sort of understanding of the impact their offences have on their victims, as well as helping them acquire the skills which they need to live good and satisfying lives so that they are less likely to continue offending.

The success rate of such programmes is still debated, but evidence from some studies shows that convictions for re-offending can be reduced significantly by a well-designed and well-implemented programme.

Changed behaviour is possible for some, though how far it is 'control' rather than 'cure', is a subject of debate.

In recent years, following a model of caring for a small number of sex-offenders on their release into the community, developed in Canada, the Quaker Peace and Social Witness group set up a support scheme in the Thames Valley Area. 'Circles of Support and Accountability' has been a highly effective community response to reducing re-offending by some sex offenders, described as medium to high risk. Circles is based on restorative justice principles (see p. 230). Circles are groups of people from the community who are fully trained, supported and supervised to work with offenders on their release from prison. The offender, known as the Core Member, is supported by volunteers who meet with him and provide help to establish an independent life. Crucially, however, the Core Member is accountable to the supporting group. Effective partnership is key to success. The Circles work with the police, the probation service and the prison service, as well as those involved in MAPPA (Multi Agency Public Protection Arrangements). In almost six years none of the offenders with whom the first pilot scheme worked, has committed a further sexual offence. Circles are now starting to be delivered in other parts of the country, and by other agencies.

> *Lord God,*
> *we hold in your presence*
> *all who distort your image*
> *in their distortion of childhood.*
>
> *We hold in your presence*
> *those whose lack of self-esteem*
> *and understanding*
> *drives them to violate*
> *the bodies of children.*
> *We hold in your presence*
> *the brokenness and bitterness*
> *of those whose innocence*
> *has been destroyed.*
>
> *We hold in your presence*
> *those who seek to bring*
> *healing and wholeness*
> *in word and deed,*
> *confident of a resurrection story.*

Information
For more information on 'Circles', please visit www.circles-uk.org

Sex-offenders and religion

Ivan had been convicted of a serious sexual offence. He had also 'found religion' in a big way, shortly after his conviction – in a simple way, which brokered no discussion. What I was presented with was 'the new man'; the 'old' had been discarded, along with his victim. The offence no longer mattered – that had been committed by the 'old' man – and this 'new creation in Christ' was somebody different.

Such a firm conviction, black and white, is common in some offenders, and in some sex-offenders in particular. When it happens, and when the past is denied in this way, it is very difficult for chaplains, or any member of staff, to break through the facade which hides the reality which is the person. The use of common religious language with chaplains, volunteers and others, may be one way of eliciting sympathy and understanding without it being realised by those people.

Ivan had come from a deeply religious family and occasionally such families may distort religious teaching in order to instil a fear of human sexuality in their children. When he was offered the chance to attend the Sex Offender Treatment Programme, Ivan declined, saying, 'I don't need to do anything like that. I've found the answer to my problems. Jesus and the Bible meet all my needs. Jesus has taken care of my problem.'

A preoccupation with reading his Bible, preparing a prayer-letter to send to sympathetic people throughout the country, and responding to their encouragement, meant he was 'cocooned' in a religious world where being 'born again' meant an alternative reality.

Any of my attempts to help him face up to his situation were met by rejection. 'You're not even a Christian,' he would say. 'When were you born again?' Any reply was never accepted.

On one occasion, when I refused one of his requests, I was threatened physically.

And when it was known that I was to leave that prison, his prayer-letter carried a request for people to pray for 'a real Christian chaplain, unlike the one we have now.'

Ivan's credibility amongst those who received his prayer-letter and who read his letters in many Christian publications, was enormous. His accounts of his 'work for the Lord' in prison led many Christians to give thanks for his ministry.

Two years later he was accused of the rape of a fellow member of the prison congregation.

Chaplains, volunteers and Christians in the wider community are seen by some sex-offenders as offering acceptance and forgiveness at any price. But there is a price, and it may be high. All who minister in prison need to be aware of their potential to be 'abused', and must not collude with, distort or minimise the offences of those with whom they work.

Chaplains have a unique role to play in contributing to the faith-understanding and world-view of prisoners. Some chaplains work with sex-offenders in small groups, helping them to come to terms with their offences in the light of their faith. Through support and understanding they can enable prisoners to come to a point where they will take part in the Sex Offender Treatment Programme, and give ongoing support. With some prisoners they can explore spiritual practice and an understanding of belonging to a faith community, and how, correctly managed, that can be a help on release. They can contribute to the success or failure of those who see religion as a cover for the past. This work demands rigour, self-understanding and training.

> Would not God discover this? For he knows the secrets of the heart.
>
> Psalm 44:21

God of understanding,
we distort our conception of you

if we offer 'cheap grace'.
Help us to provide support
with challenge,
hope with realism,
encouragement with insight,
integrity with compassion.

Almighty God
to whom all hearts are open,
all desires known,
and from whom no secrets are hidden:
cleanse the thoughts of our hearts
by the inspiration of your Holy Spirit,
that we may perfectly love you,
and worthily magnify your holy name;
through Christ our Lord.

Common Worship, Order One

Vulnerable prisoners – Rule 45

I'm rarely in the prison on a Saturday. On this occasion I had made an exception, for an ecumenical group of church people coming in to learn about the context and practice of prison ministry.

As I sat in the office, putting the final touches to what I was going to say, the phone rang. An articulate woman told me that her father, over 80 years of age, had been sentenced to four years the day before. He was, she said, 'in a terrible state', and had been told immediately that he would be going to a prison for convicted prisoners many miles from his home, despite there being one much nearer, and more convenient for visits and the maintenance of relationships. Having been given my name by her vicar, she was now asking me a huge number of questions on behalf of her mother and her father. Gradually, I tried to fit the pieces together, and when she told me her father's location within the prison, the situation became clearer.

Ernest was on 'D' Wing, the Vulnerable Prisoner Unit, otherwise known as the Rule 45 Wing or, in the language of most other prisoners, the 'nonces' wing'. Not all of the 33 men held there are sex-offenders, but the assumption is that they are. They are all there for their own protection, and have usually requested to be 'on the Rule'. Some have allegedly committed sex-offences, or have been recently convicted of having done so; some have got themselves into debt with other prisoners, perhaps drug- or gambling-related, and, unable to pay, have sought refuge away from the other wings. Given that Ernest had only come into prison the previous evening, I could rule out his being in the latter group. I assured his daughter I would see him as soon as possible and would find answers to some of her questions.

As I arrived in the Unit, Ernest was being 'signed' up by a member of the Independent Monitoring Board, who are required to visit all Rule 45 prisoners within their first 72 hours, and to make sure they want to be 'on the Rule'. Ernest and I sat in the Library, observing the usual rules whereby I could be seen by an officer, but we could not be overheard in conversation. Such a rule, for the safety of staff, seemed unnecessary in this instance, but had to be obeyed. Ernest called me 'Padre', and despite my time in the Royal Air Force, where it was constantly used, it's a form of address that I find 'grates' with me. Within a very short time, however, Ernest had revealed much of himself, and without prompting, spoke of the reasons for his conviction, whilst strongly protesting his innocence and denying the offences.

Ernest spoke quietly, deliberately, with great clarity, and a sense of deep hurt at being in such a place for the first time, subjected as he had been the previous evening to taunts of 'beast', 'monster', 'nonce', 'child molester'. Unlike some on the wing, he had only experienced verbal abuse, not physical. He had not been spat at, had urine thrown at him or poured under his door, had his food interfered with, or been hit. For even here there is a 'pecking order' which seeks to 'grade' offences and to make scapegoats of those considered by some prisoners to have done something more reprehensible than they themselves have done.

I was deeply touched by his story, and I tried, as ever, not to judge, but to listen and to try to help him in whatever way was appropriate. As with his daughter, he was deeply troubled by the prospect of being in a prison so far from home, though he knew that the commitment of his wife and daughter would ensure that they visited. But he had discovered why he would not be nearer home. It had been explained to him just before my arrival. He had been convicted of sexual offences, and the prison to which he wanted to go would accept him on its sex-offender wing, but only if he acknowledge his guilt. He would not, and refused to compromise his integrity by saying he was guilty, even though it would have made his visits easier, and may even have helped him to be released a little earlier. As I left, he said, 'Say a prayer with me, Padre.'

Later, I was able to confirm with a staff member in the Observation, Classification and Allocation group that his explanation was correct. I phoned his daughter. By midday on Monday he had gone, but not to the prison of his choice. This was a reminder of the immediacy of ministry in such a place, of having to make instant relationships which, hopefully, reflect something of God's love. Sometimes, there are no second chances.

Just a few weeks later, I spoke to another man, Kenneth. He was in the Health Centre, his face bandaged, his hands encased in protective plastic, hiding burns caused by boiling water that had been poured over him. His waist area was heavily bandaged, following many kicks. Kenneth had declined the opportunity to 'go on the numbers' (i.e. to be a Rule 45 prisoner), and had remained on normal location for some weeks without anyone knowing the nature of his offence. With just ten days to go before his release, some of those on his landing discovered why he was inside. A distorted and perverted form of 'justice' had been enacted, harshly and with incredible speed. It had been well orchestrated and was over in minutes.

In Court he had pleaded his innocence. On the landing, he had no second chance. The 'scapegoating' of others is a common coping mechanism used by some prisoners to divert attention from themselves, to avoid the need for self-examination. It is a cowardly action, but it can exact a high cost, as Kenneth discovered.

Do not judge so that you may not be judged.

Matthew 7:1

See what love the Father has given us, that we should be called children of God; and that is what we are.

1 John 3:1

Lord, your Son reached out
to the scapegoats of his time,
and those on the margins;
we hold before you
all who are isolated
as vulnerable prisoners;
those who live with
mockery, insult, and alienation;
so often regarded as less than human.
As we affirm the worth
of all your children,
so help us to foster
self-worth, dignity, and respect
in those who are vulnerable.

We pray for the staff
who work in such units,
for the patience to care
for the impatient and demanding,
for their ability to see
beyond the offence,
to the person.

Foreign nationals

Chaplains, and other members of staff, sometimes experience the re-roleing of a prison – from holding one category of prisoner to another, sometimes from male to female, or vice versa. In this story the prison had moved from holding prisoners on remand from court to holding only foreign nationals.

'Reduce prison numbers – send foreign nationals home', proclaim some newspapers. I really dislike the term 'foreign national'! My ministry, as a Chaplain, has at its heart the 'love your neighbour' ethos, and I cannot get my head around those two phrases which seem to be completely at odds with each other.

How can I love my neighbour if I consider him to be alien? 'Foreign national', as a term, suggests that we do not belong together, that there is a natural alienation. Whereas 'international' is inclusive and has a whole different feel to it. So, I am officially a Chaplain to a foreign national prison but I consider myself as belonging to an international community.

And that is exactly what we are in this prison – a meeting-place for over 65 nationalities. Throughout the prison service there are about 11,000 people from 169 countries, classed as foreign nationals (non-UK passport holders). We speak in even more languages and represent widely differing cultures, religions and traditions. It is such an exciting place to work in. The place buzzes with variety. Even the board-games are intriguing and include things like Xianggi (from China), Gwat Pai (from Canton) and Gomoku (from Japan).

Understanding one another is a steep learning curve. Things we take for granted have to be reconsidered. For example, if I give the thumbs-up sign to an Englishman, he will smile and, hopefully, feel encouraged, whereas the same sign to an

Algerian will be insulting and have quite the opposite effect! It isn't only the spoken language that can be misunderstood.

Chaplains of all the faith traditions have been encouraged by the depth of worship in services and meetings within prisons. The world, it seems, is still very keen to practise the faith they belong to. This has made it less of a struggle to keep the sacred areas in chaplaincy clean and respected! If I take prayer seriously, I am likely to empathise with another's need to do likewise. Our worship areas then are truly holy places and no one room is used exclusively by any one group. We share. So, for instance, the large worship hall is a church on Sundays, a Muslim prayer room on Fridays and a Buddhist prayer room on a Thursday. The quiet, peaceful atmosphere in that place is created by the prayers and meditations of all who use it.

The ethos of 'love your neighbour', common to all world faiths, is worked out within these prison walls. People of different backgrounds, religions, cultures and languages have to live together, and they are an example to the world outside of how peaceful co-existence may be a dream, but a dream that can be fulfilled. We use the symbol of a rainbow to express the deeply held belief in a vision that we can change the world. The colours can stand alone and they have their own depth and richness, but together and only together, they form a stunning arc of contrasts, a bow that depends on each brilliant hue connecting with the others and so becoming interdependent. It is about accepting our differences and not feeling threatened by them. It is about honouring and valuing every human being, whatever their faith or creed, and following the maxim of doing unto others what we would like done to ourselves. When the time comes to return to the country of their birth, the message will travel with those who have had a first-hand experience of tolerance and harmony. Inevitably that message will influence those they next share their lives with.

As Chaplains we have the duty and responsibility to not only accept the faith of others, but to ensure that we enable all to worship freely, safely and with dignity. But our ministry extends far beyond the spiritual. We are pastors to all who live and work within the prison. With the daily worries and concerns of those awaiting possible deportation, whose family live not only miles away but halfway round the globe, and for whom English is a foreign, unintelligible language, fear and anxiety are all-consuming worries. The waiting-to-know can be intolerable and the decisions often unpalatable. Chaplains and other staff have their work cut out to reassure and encourage. Finding hope can be an up-hill task and there are times when, humanly speaking, hope is beyond our reach. Platitudes are easy to give but have no value, and it is hard to sit in a cell with someone whose future is increasingly bleak. It is comforting to me when I can be of comfort but hugely frustrating when I am helpless to offer anything except my time, company and helplessness, and it is all too easy to assume I understand the situation that person faces. I try to walk in the shoes of my brother but actually, the truth may be, he does not walk in shoes at all in his motherland and I have absolutely no idea what it is like to live in his home, his land, his culture and his religion.

I think of the man who tried to hang himself because a member of his family was a close supporter of a dictator. He was terrified of going back to his home country for fear of reprisals now that the dictator has been deposed.

Then there was the man whose parents, brothers and sisters were all killed in a coup, and he was left with grief oozing from every pore of his being. He had a girlfriend in this country but his life was overshadowed by the loss of his family. His pain was tangible, excruciating and simply heart-breaking. Our need was to make him feel better, but that was patronising, and we had to accept that perhaps he needed to be allowed to feel that raw agony, to 'keen' for his loved ones, to enter into their suffering somehow through his own.

Another man had come to this country so he could have drugs to treat his epilepsy, because he could not get them in his homeland. He too wanted to earn enough money to buy his new bride a home and intended to return to her within two years, but he ended up committing a crime, was jailed and sent home with nothing. He was desperate that the two years had been wasted and that he also faced a grim future as a serious epileptic, with no medicine, no support and in a society that saw the illness as evil. He wasn't welcome here but he wasn't welcome there either.

Of course, there are some happy endings, and one of our recent Christian prisoners has cheerfully returned home to Africa, unafraid, a future laid out for him and family to welcome him back. The International Organisation for Migration which is funded by 150 governments has also begun working with prisons to help resettle people and to ensure that deportees don't return to nothing. They help them find work or start a business, find accommodation, even education for their children. Field Workers around the world give support and encouragement until roots are established and the returning man (or woman) is settled.

Every day has its sadness, its challenges and its sense of rich variety. Today, for instance, we have welcomed Sikhs to their meeting with a cheery 'Sat Sri Akal', whilst the orderly busied himself converting the prayer hall for Muslim prayers. As the Sikh chaplain left with a 'Merry Christmas' to his Christian colleagues, 50 Muslims were welcomed with the traditional 'Assalamu alaikum' and the hand-on-heart gesture that signifies, 'I really mean this! It's from the heart!' As the Muslim chaplain began his sermon, the Rabbi arrived, and after lunch, his flock were greeted with a warm 'Shalom'. In between, 12 new receptions were seen, the Segregation Unit was visited, a member of staff was counselled and a Review on a vulnerable prisoner was attended. An Eastern European who has had some fascinating tales to tell leaves on the bus to a detention centre and a chaplain attends the daily briefing. The Muslim, Jewish and Free Church chaplains gather to discuss the local Interfaith Movement, and a visit is organised with Epafras, a Dutch prisoner support organisation. Just another Friday!

A radio interview of our Chaplaincy went out last week and one of our Muslim prisoners told the reporter, 'I am very lucky to be here. This is a good place to be.' I would echo that sentiment wholeheartedly. What a rich experience it is to be involved with people from around the world. We have so much to give and receive from each other, so much we can learn. Chaplaincy gives each new detainee a bookmark that says:

> Our first task in approaching another people, another culture, another religion, is to take off our shoes, for the place we are approaching is holy, otherwise we may find ourselves treading on another's dreams![15]

This is a place that can change the world if we can but learn to tread carefully. It is certainly a place of dreams, and reality!

> *God of love, and of life,*
> *may we tread carefully*
> *as we walk through this life.*
> *May we walk together,*
> *arm in arm,*
> *as friends.*
> *May we offer a smile before a frown,*
> *the hand of peace instead of the fist of fear.*
> *May we one day*
> *dare to share our dreams*
> *beneath the rainbow of love.*

Seeking asylum

Rachel stood in the chaplaincy office. 'OK, then. I'll do a deal with you. I won't cut up any more while I'm here, 'cos you people been good to me. But when I get off the plane back home, and walk out of the airport, I will walk out in front of the fastest car, killing myself, and my baby.' An uncertain future weighed heavily on her heart and mind.

Rachel was an illegal immigrant from an East African country, where she lived in poverty and disillusionment. She had endured the trauma of rape, keeping her baby and arriving in the UK, determined to make a future for them both. Isolated and afraid, she bought a National Insurance number, gained work, but cashed a cheque intended for the rightful owner of the same National Insurance number. Imprisoned, and seeking asylum, it was clear that she would be deported, her situation not helped by her criminal act. Rachel, and her baby, are HIV positive.

Rachel is well supported by members of the chaplaincy team, by other staff members, by a strong network of other women, who meet together daily for prayer and praise in the prison chapel, and by a volunteer. Many seek to understand their lives, and their imprisonment, in religious terms. They ask difficult questions about the nature of justice, the purpose of suffering, as they seek to give spiritual meaning to lives lived in a way most of us would find hard to imagine, let alone bear. Faith can provide that meaning, giving an ultimate hope. It can be a journey like no other, for people whose journey has rarely been positive. Perhaps, for Rachel, too ...

Rachel will spend more time in prison before being transferred to a Removal Centre, operated by the Border and Immigration Agency. There are ten Removal Centres in the UK, with spaces for 2724 people, referred to as 'immigration detainees'. They can be asylum seekers who have arrived legally and whose claims are being investigated; people who have not arrived legally; over-stayers who have not returned home when their visa has expired; criminals awaiting deportation; or refused asylum seekers awaiting removal.

The effects of detention, be it in removal centres, or in prison, are significant, leading, for some, to feelings of isolation, low self-esteem and depressive behaviour. The stress of protracted legal proceedings, particularly as the date of removal approaches, can lead to hopelessness and despair. The risk of self-harm and suicide attempts increases.

In the midst of a potentially overwhelming atmosphere of despair, chaplains, staff and volunteers seek to ameliorate some of the effects of detention. Formed in 1994, the Association of Visitors to Immigration Detainees (AVID), with 450 volunteers from 27 groups, seeks to support individuals and groups who visit some of those detained. Very often AVID volunteers are the only person a detainee may see who is not an 'official'. Volunteers offer one-to-one support, often listening to extraordinary stories of torture or tragedy. One detainee said: 'When I hear my name being called – to receive a visitor – it is a cause of celebration.'

> For there is no distinction between Jew and Greek; the same Lord is Lord of all and is generous to all who call on him.
>
> Romans 10:12

Gracious
and generous God,
you have called us
to celebrate
life-giving love
in your Son.

Yet for many,
celebration may

be hard won
and costly.

Enable us to
hold to the vision
of your love, even in the
painful experience of life,
that through it we
may be transformed,
and know your presence.

Information

The Home Office has announced that a further 1300–1500 additional places will be available in Removal Centres by 2012.
www.bia.homeoffice.gov.uk
www.aviddetention.org.uk

REFLECTIVE THEMES

Evil

Questions about evil are an inevitable aspect of every thinking person's life. In the prison context the questions arise frequently. Some people find it tempting to give easy answers, from a psychological or theological point of view. I do not believe there are any such answers.

The piece which follows was written by David Wilson, formerly a prison governor and now a Professor of Criminology. David, a Christian, provides insight into some aspects of the concept of evil. He has had a wide experience of the prison service, and he bases some of his thoughts on his relationships with prisoners labelled 'evil'. I have added a biblical reference and a prayer, with David's permission.

'Apartment 213 contained seven skulls, and four heads, three in the standing freezer, and one in a box on the bottom shelf of the refrigerator. In the freezer compartment of the refrigerator there were assorted body parts. In a blue fifty-seven gallon barrel there were headless torsos, hands and assorted limbs. There were also more than a hundred photographs of people taken at various stages of dismemberment, most so disgusting that even seasoned police officials could not look at them without feeling faint.'

Why do people do appalling things to each other? How do we explain the wanton destruction of life? Should our search for explanations begin with psychology, psychiatry, genetics, or a range of environmental and social factors? To many people such a search is merely an elaborate charade, aimed at finding excuses to forgive those whom only God can forgive. The Nazis who ran concentration camps, Pol Pot in Cambodia, serial killers and rapists, the Moors Murderers and others like them – for this group of people, the argument runs, who inflict pain and suffering without apparent reason, we don't have to look too far or too deeply for an explanation – they are Evil.

This seems to have been the view of a Milwaukee Court which, a few years ago, sentenced Jeffrey Dahmer, the serial killer and occupant of Apartment 213 mentioned above, to 15 consecutive life sentences for the murders of 17 young men. Despite his own explanation of mental illness, like Peter Sutcliffe and Dennis Nilsen before him, the judicial process preferred to see him sane, ascribe responsibility for his crimes, and thus find him 'guilty'. The fact that Sutcliffe and Ian Brady, one of the Moors Murderers, are now diagnosed as paranoid schizophrenics, does not seem to have affected the judicial judgements about them, and nor do many people care, it would seem. The moral and legal problems associated with judging people who do appalling things to other human beings are presented as rather arcane philosophical musings, interesting and academic, but with little role to play in the pragmatic matter of protecting the public through incarceration. However, pragmatism often leads to corners being cut, and a shorthand being used which aims to label, rather than to understand. One such label is 'Evil'.

What follows is not intended to be a definitive analysis of Evil. Rather, it is a series of observations and thoughts about how others have used this word, and in what circumstances they have applied it to people, or events. Thus, I move rapidly from individual examples of people who have been described as evil, to historical or contemporary movements or circumstances. Inevitably this results in a patchwork, or collage, as opposed to something seamless, and I am conscious that the use of the word 'Evil' and its application differs dramatically in effect when applied to the Holocaust or, for example, when it is applied to someone who physically or sexually abuses a child. However, it is precisely because the label has been applied so randomly that such connections are interesting, if only to question the validity of the label itself, or broaden our understanding of Evil.

The word Evil is, of course, associated with our dualistic

Christian notions of Heaven and Hell, God and the Devil, and for thousands of years many people have been prepared to explain the wickedness of others in theological terms. Evil in this context is an independent force, operating with a mind of its own, seeking out converts with similar zeal to the 'Powers of Good'. (We are all familiar with the phrase, 'the devil has the best tunes', which implies something of the supposed glamour and magnetism of this 'Dark side'.) Yet in the course of my job, when I have had to work with notorious murderers and serial killers, people who have already been labelled as 'Evil' by those who have never met them, I have never once felt that this description, applied in this way, was accurate, meaningful or important. Perhaps in the same way that hand-to-hand combat, where one's opponent or victim is seen, is usually less terrible and destructive than using weapons which kill over hundreds of miles, so closeness to people who do wicked things allows one to grasp a complexity which distance denies. For Evil is not something which is separate and dynamic in itself, but rather something which is part of us all.

Some might complain that whilst this is all good and well, it does little to explain destructive and wicked acts, and cruel and unthinking violence. If Evil is part of us all, why does this shadow manifest itself in only a few, and in what circumstances? Can it really be possible that the most mild-mannered amongst us, given the right mix of factors, could turn into a monster, bent on death and destruction? Serial killers themselves find the answer to this question bewildering.

As Dennis Nilsen put it, 'No one wants to believe ever that I am just an ordinary man come to an extraordinary and overwhelming conclusion.' The steps that led him to that conclusion have been followed meticulously by Brian Masters, from Nilsen's lonely, unloved childhood, through his 11 years in the Army Catering Corps (where he learned his butchering skills), to his brief spell as a policeman, and finally to his days in the Kentish Town Jobcentre, and his nights in various gay bars. Masters concludes that Nilsen killed for company, 'to have someone to talk to, someone to care for', and that Nilsen was 'not a stranger amongst us [but rather] an extreme instance of human possibility'. What is it that makes this possible?

As psychiatrist Anthony Storr has observed, human beings are very destructive towards each other. Here I would not wish to enter into the debates about the acceptable use of aggression, whether aggression is innate or learned behaviour, nor to deny that aggression can sometimes be a positive act. What interests me instead is at what point aggression becomes translated into destructive violence.

It has been calculated that between 1820 and 1945, 59 million people died in Europe as a result of war, murder or other acts of violence, and in particular in Auschwitz alone, at the height of the Second World War, 6000 Jews, Poles, Russians, Gypsies, homosexuals and others were exterminated each day. Closer to home, the National Society for the Prevention of Cruelty to Children calculates that 200 children each year die in Britain at the hands of their parents, or step-parents, and Childline, established to deal with the overwhelming reality of child abuse, receives thousands of calls each year.

The growing awareness of those who work with sex-offenders that there is a cycle of abuse, in which those who are abused as children may go on themselves to abuse when mature, suggests something of the enormous importance of childhood in the development of individual personality and behaviour. Childhood is for far too many a baptism of fire, burning psychological scars deep into the unconscious. I have already alluded to Nilsen's unhappy childhood growing up in Fraserburgh, and similarly Peter Sutcliffe, who nearly died during labour, was a sickly, sensitive boy, who was regularly bullied at school. Nilsen's and Sutcliffe's childhood experiences are not uncommon, and instances of the horrific treatment of children who, unlike them, never survive beyond infancy are numerous and disturbing. I hope that two examples will suffice.

Some years ago, *The Independent* newspaper reported the trial in Bristol of David Hammond, who killed his daughter by beating her with his fists, then a ruler, plastic tubing and a kettle-flex, before picking her up by the hair, and throwing her into the bath. In the same year Danny Palmer killed his seven-month-old stepson by beating him about the head with a rounders bat, causing extensive bleeding to the baby's eyes and lacerations to his mouth. The post-mortem also revealed that both the baby's arms had been broken just above the wrist. Does all this put some perspective on the 'Moors Murderers', Ian Brady and Myra Hindley, who bizarrely taped the screams and pleas of their young victims to 'mummy and daddy', a transcript of which controversially formed the conclusion of Gordon Burn's novel *Alma Cogan*?

Children, who by their very nature are helpless and dependent, are thus ironically also the centre of their household. The reality of their inability to fend for themselves automatically places total responsibility for their well-being onto others, establishing new domestic hierarchies and priorities. Some insecure adults find this threatening to their self-esteem, or may feel themselves replaced in their partner's affections, and if they themselves have been badly treated or abused as children, or made to feel worthless, the recipe for disaster becomes all the more apparent. What this serves to underscore is the importance of adopting a positive, rather than a punitive approach to children, and providing the necessary support to those parents who require help, in the form of child benefit allowances, crèche facilities, and nursery care. The link between childhood experience and adult behaviour is complex, especially since many of the most disadvantaged or abused children go on to make outstanding contributions to our society, never dreaming of treating their own offspring cruelly, but it is nonetheless surely true to argue that children who are loved and cared for in a stable environment, are going to be themselves in a better position to love and care for others in the years to come.

It is worthwhile to reflect on the childhood and personality of Jeffrey Dahmer, especially given the seemingly similar patterns of development that we are now aware of between Dahmer and Dennis Nilsen. Dahmer was brought up in a middle-class household where his parents spent much of their time arguing. His childhood was characterised by isolation and neglect. He had no close friends, and gradually withdrew into a fantasy world of his own making. When he was 12 his parents divorced, and his mother left home with his younger brother David, leaving him to be looked after by his father. He eventually enrolled in Ohio State University, but dropped out after one semester, and thereafter enlisted in the Army. Colleagues from his Army days remember that he was a 'different man' when he had been drinking, and Dahmer drank constantly, which eventually led to his dismissal. From the Army he gained employment in the Ambrosia Chocolate Company, where he worked until his arrest, and spent his evenings in Milwaukee's gay bars.

There is much in all this which is common to Dennis Nilsen. Both drank to excess, had had careers in the Army, were homosexual and personable enough to 'pick up' their victims. Of greater interest were their similar childhood experiences, characterised by isolation and loneliness and being abandoned by those whom they loved. In Nilsen's case his beloved grandfather died, and in Dahmer's his parents' divorce resulted in his mother leaving home. Dahmer was later to claim that it was his dislike of being left alone that led him to kill his first victim, a hitch-hiker to whom he had offered a lift. Both used to take photographs of their victims, partly as a masturbatory device, kept body parts in their house and would seem to have existed in a fantasy world, partly formed by alcohol abuse, in which power, control and status, denied to them in reality, were theirs for the moment.

De-personalising as a means of subjugation or gaining acquiescence is a common device employed by 'total institutions'. On reception into prison, for example, the first thing that will happen to you is that your personal clothing will be taken from you, and you will be provided with a uniform. You will be asked to bathe (symbolically washing away the 'outside world'), given a number (symbolic of the new 'inside world' you have joined), and informed of a set of rules which place you at the bottom of a hierarchy in which you have no control and little power. Individual personality becomes subsumed by a group identity, and a system of life is established dependent not upon personal preference, but on the needs of the organisation. When the needs of the organisation take priority over the needs of the individual, abuse is inevitable, allowing custodians to justify ill treatment as a consequence of the need for 'efficiency', 'economy', or other, similar rationalisations.

The examples above, of cruelty and destruction, come from deep within the imaginations of Man. The ability to see others as less than human, to rank them according to perceived status, creed, sex or colour, stems from a conscious capacity to analyse and think. The development of ideologies, the choosing of options or courses of action on the basis of that analysis, is the necessary prelude to violent behaviour. Imagination, Man's greatest asset, is also his Achilles' heel. To see another as evil requires an imaginative capacity not found in animals, and it is Man's capacity for abstract thought, his ability to give meaning and purpose to his life, incorporating the knowledge of his own ultimate death, which elevates him beyond the animal world. It is his discontent with the way the world is which gives him mastery of it, but that mastery has to be tempered by reason. But reason is often the first casualty when tempers fly, or tongues or fists are loosened by alcohol, or when one group or individual wants to feel more important or valued by asserting superiority over another. Of course, imagination cannot be controlled, but it can be shaped and moulded, given the proper circumstances.

Significantly, both Dennis Nilsen and Jeffrey Dahmer inhabited a fantasy world of their own making, and in another context sex therapists have drawn attention to the power of fantasy as a prelude to sexual assault. These fantasies invariably place the protagonist in a position of power and importance. Thus, in this respect we could end cruelty and wickedness tomorrow by beginning to value all who live in our world, regardless of their size, their sex, their colour, their religion, or political affiliation. Undoubtedly this aspiration is a forlorn hope, but if we start by recognising that no one is 'evil', separately, totally, dynamically, and that instead the roots of wickedness are in us all, we may at least begin to grasp the way forward.

I consider that the sufferings of this present time are not worth comparing with the glory about to be revealed to us. For the creation waits with eager longing for the revealing of the children of God; for the creation was subjected to futility, not of its own will but by the will of the one who subjected it, in hope that the creation itself will be set free from its bondage to decay and will obtain the freedom of the glory of the children of God. We know that the whole creation has been groaning in labour pains until now; and not only the creation, but we ourselves, who have the first fruits of the Spirit, groan inwardly while we wait for adoption, the redemption of our bodies. For in hope we were saved. Now hope that is seen is not hope. For who hopes for what is seen? But if we hope for what we do not see, we wait for it with patience.

Romans 8:18–25

Lord of all creation,
in acknowledgement of our
capacity for evil,
we are silent before you.

The silence of despair
can overwhelm us
as we reflect on our ability
to mar your image,
and to walk in the path of self-destruction.

Fill us with faithfulness,
with a 'groaning' –
a quiet cry – which

enables us to contemplate
in redemptive silence.

May we be filled with hope in Christ,
in the power of the Spirit,
and in the certainty of a vision
for your future glory.

This prayer was inspired by some words from
Embodying Forgiveness by L. Gregory Jones

Anger

Alby is 29 years of age, a life-sentence prisoner. He has done ten years in prison for manslaughter and, at the time of writing, was on a course of therapy in Grendon Prison, a therapeutic community. Alby provides us with an insight into one who has perpetrated physical violence. It is easy to be outraged at such acts, difficult to begin to understand what may be behind them. Understanding will never of itself lead to solutions, but it does provide us with a glimpse of ourselves. Alby concludes his piece with a deeply personal prayer, to which I have added a more general one.

Lord, I cried out to you last night. I said, 'God help me,' and I felt nothing. Maybe I didn't feel you with me when I prayed because I don't deserve you. I wanted to feel some spark within myself. I wanted to hear words like 'Yes, I love you.' I wanted to feel your arms around me. I felt nothing.

I cried last night in my cell, and I've never cried in my cell like that before. It's make-or-break time for me. I got through it before because I was stoned. Now that's not possible.

Lord, I'm not a monster. I'm a good man who did a very bad thing. *I know what I've done.* I stabbed a woman 15 times, to death. I heard her pleas and I ignored them. I know that. That's here in my heart. *I know what I've done.* Sometimes I feel like writing to the Court of Appeal to say, 'Can you give me another ten years on my sentence?'

I was up from 12 to 4 in the morning with suicide thoughts. I said I would kill myself at 29 because my mother was 29 when she killed herself. I thought, 'I'll give these people something to think about.' I can't, of course. I've got people who mean something to me, and I think if I kill myself I'd be a lost soul.

I'm sick to death of these cold callous people who pass

judgement on me. I want to get hold of these people because (God forgive me) they are cruel. Now I've got two more years of having to say, 'I'm a sex-offender. What objectives have you got for me?'

They don't know what life is like. They were just little talcum-powdered kids; then they went to college.[17] It's wrong to think like this. I don't really like myself seeing them as scum-bags. But I've been raped in prison one hundred thousand times by their questions.

In 1989, if you'd let me out, you'd have had a serial killer. Now I don't want to hurt people. *I know what I've done.* I've left untold numbers of victims.

But I'm sick of it. There's a human being here.

O God, you know the frustrations I feel and the difficulties I go through as a human being. You know my heart and true desire. In the midst of all this, I pray.

> *Lord, your Son was not afraid*
> *to express his anger.*
> *Help us to voice ours,*
> *to own that which may*
> *provoke us to verbal*
> *or physical reaction.*
> *As we seek to understand*
> *the 'self', enable us to acknowledge*
> *what we are before you,*
> *in order that we might become*
> *what you would have us be.*

Remorse, or repentance?

'He shows no remorse,' said the probation officer at the meeting where a multi-disciplinary team was discussing the regular progress reports, which are written every three years to assess the progress of life-sentence prisoners.

I chose to disagree, not because I thought the assessment was wrong, for Brian did not appear to exhibit remorse. I believed he had moved beyond that stage. How long can one expect people to go on showing remorse? When is it more than just a learned response, or an appropriate response, to satisfy the needs of the report writer?

Brian had been in prison for a long time. He knew what to say, when to say it. We had spent many hours together and my initial revulsion of what this otherwise likeable man had done had long since passed. Or so I thought. Re-reading his record, with its details of the offence, I was forced to question my own assessment. But I went with my heart.

How could I justify or even explain my difference of understanding to the probation officer and my other colleagues? Brian was not particularly religious and only occasionally attended chapel, but what he was now manifesting in his life was, I felt, repentance, not remorse. It is a distinction worth reflection. Is remorse any more than regret, or self-blame for an action? Something which can be acknowledged without having to think about giving up a previous way of life? Something which can easily lose its 'bite' with the passage of time and become merely an uncomfortable memory?

Repentance is something different. It is about *metanoia*, a reorientation of the personality, a renunciation of a particular way of life, or thinking. It may be the start of transformation, a radical change of perspective which does not require that the past be negated, or rejected, but which involves a new perception, a re-cognition of that past. And it is, I feel, more acceptable in the prison context than conversion, which too often can mean such a 'swing in the pendulum' that there is a chasm, a rupture, between past and present, with a refusal to accept the reality of that past.

Others were not convinced. Christian language, religious language, and understanding is sometimes counter-cultural and not understood, or accepted. Particularly amongst those who seek only to satisfy the desire for retribution. Six years later, Brian faces yet another review.

> Rend your hearts and not your clothing.
> Return to the Lord, your God,
> for he is gracious and merciful,
> slow to anger, and abounding
> in steadfast love,
> and relents from punishing.

Joel 2:13

God may perhaps grant that they will repent and come to know the truth.

2 Timothy 2:25

Do you not realize that God's kindness is meant to lead you to repentance?

Romans 2:4b

> *God of mercy,*
> *our words express*
> *our beliefs about you,*
> *our understanding of*
> *your grace and love*
> *in the lives of all your people.*
> *In our care for others*
> *help us to be careful*
> *in our use of language,*
> *that we may show forth*
> *your kindness, and through it,*
> *lead people to repentance.*

Race matters

Johnston was in the Health Centre Treatment Room. His skin, scalded by boiling water mixed with sugar, hung from one side of his face, neck and shoulder. His blackness was only skin deep; his burns and pain were exposed and raw.

Later, in the quiet of the Chapel, he spoke of what could only be described as a racist attack by another prisoner. 'Every day of my life I've been subject to abuse from white people. I've never set foot outside my front door one day without racist remarks.' But he steadfastly refused to make a complaint: 'It ain't worth it – I'd get worse than this, probably.'

Black African and Black Caribbean prisoners make up about 15 per cent of the prison population. About 27 per cent of all prisoners, including seven per cent who are Asian, are from Black or Minority Ethnic (BME) groups, which is a disproportionate number, given that eight per cent of the wider community are from BME groups (Black, two per cent; Asian, four per cent). Some 29 per cent of women prisoners are from BME groups. Whilst one of the reasons for the high number of black female prisoners is involvement in the importation of drugs, and even when foreign nationals are excluded, the number of black people in prison still remains disproportionate.

Race matters.

Johnston, at 23 years of age, had been in trouble with the law for the first time. But he was no more likely to have committed an offence than a young white adult. Unlike his white counterparts, he was less likely to have been involved in the use of illegal drugs. He was three-and-a-half times more likely to be arrested than a white youth and he was six times more likely to go to prison for his offence than a white person. Prison population statistics indicate that black people who commit offences are more likely to end up in prison than comparable white offenders, and with longer sentences. Yet black people coming into prison have fewer convictions than white prisoners.

Race matters.

Johnston told me of the many times he had been stopped and searched by the police in his late teenage years and until his imprisonment. Living within the Metropolitan Police area of London, he was seven times more likely to be stopped and searched than his white friends. His Asian friends were twice as likely to be stopped and searched as his white friends.

Race matters.

Johnston's scars are deeper than the wounds I saw exposed. He feels he comes from a community which is disadvantaged, and which suffers disproportionately from poverty, poor housing, unemployment, and other forms of social deprivation.

Race matters.

In most criminal justice agencies there have been increases in the employment of people from BME groups, and the Prison Service currently employs 6.2 per cent of its staff from these groups. The Serious Fraud Office and the Youth Offending Teams have the highest BME representation. The lowest proportion of BME members is within the Judiciary, which has only a three per cent representation. The majority within this group were employed at the levels of District Judge and Recorder. There are no Lord Justices from BME groups.

Race matters.

> Then Peter began to speak to them: 'I truly understand that God shows no partiality ...'
>
> Acts 10:34

> Those who say, 'I love God', and hate their brothers or sisters, are liars ...
>
> 1 John 4:20

> *Lord, forgive us for the silence*
> *that condones injustice,*
> *withholds forgiveness,*

disguises anger,
prolongs quarrels,
breeds misunderstandings,
shows contempt,
permits ignorance,
kills love,
expresses indifference,
increases fear,
makes barriers.

We pray for the gift of love,
that we may trust and care for one another.

We pray for the gift of courage,
that we may be bold in our work and witness.

We pray for the gifts of grace,
that we may rejoice in our shared humanity.

We pray for the gift of faith,
that we might believe we will be one.

We pray that you will hold us in your care
and make us wholly yours.

I saw Johnston a few weeks later, just before his transfer to another prison. He told me the scars were healing and his skin would eventually regain its natural colour. 'I don't want to be half black and half white – I just want to be me.' For him, as for most of us, race matters.

Information
For more statistical information visit www.cjsonline.gov. uk/downloads

Confidentiality

*An Anglican chaplain in a prison with long-term prisoners writes
in this piece, and reflects in his prayer on the issue of confidentiality.
The seal of the Confessional must always remain so, but
there are many other areas relating to this matter which arise on
an almost daily basis. It is rarely an area of conflict for chaplains,
but the potential for it to be so remains.*

As a Chaplain, I am leading a regular discussion group, where
men are encouraged to 'be themselves', and to take 'time out' of
the normal prison environment. Over the weeks I notice that
one man regularly manipulates the group, despite efforts to
prevent him doing so. We often find ourselves listening to his
inappropriate jokes about women.

Later, I find myself having to write a report about this man.
Reports are written when a prisoner is coming up for consideration
for parole, or every three years for a 'Lifer'. His crime
was of violence against a woman, but his reports indicate he
has progressed well and causes no trouble in prison. The
decision I have to make relates to the area of confidentiality. Do
I reveal what I have experienced in the group, or do I allow it
to pass without comment, in which case he may progress without
further question towards release. Even if he agrees to
disclosure, it changes the nature of the group. And prisoners
need somewhere they can be relaxed and not feel 'watched' and
tested.

Issues of confidentiality arise every day. Rarely major, sometimes
trivial, they raise questions of how far chaplains are only
the receivers of information, and not the sharers. Should a
comment made in an unguarded moment, in a 'safe' environment,
be passed to staff? Most often the answer will be 'no'. It's
a risk, but as Jesus gave men and women dignity in his dealings

with them, so in following him we must hold carefully what men and women tell us as precious, and as a gift between friends, not a commodity to be traded in the market-place.

Lord, set a guard on our tongues.
Help us to know when to speak
and when to keep silence.
In such a risky business,
when we make mistakes
and should have spoken,
by your love protect those involved.
Be with all who write reports
and in other ways handle
intimate knowledge of others' lives.
Make us ever careful
with the precious gifts we hold.

On dying

In the hospice in adjacent rooms called 'Daffodil' and 'Bluebell', lay the two men. John was a prisoner, handcuffed by one arm to his bed with a chain, discreetly covered with a rug by one of the two sensitive officers. In civilian clothes now, these two officers had been in uniform for some days, attracting much attention and causing some anxiety for friends and relatives of those in the hospice, simply because of the implication of their presence. Prison regulations had demanded the wearing of uniform until relaxation could be sought on compassionate grounds.

The other man was a colleague, a member of the Chaplaincy Team, a Quaker who had been a dentist, then a Roman Catholic Deacon who had read Theology at Cambridge. A man of integrity and with a depth of compassion which meant he never failed 'to find something of God' in all whom he met. A man who loved and was loved, who had given of himself within and without the prison. The contrast was pronounced, despite their both being imprisoned by unconsciousness. John, chained to an officer, only to be 'released' with death; without family and with only one friend, himself a prisoner in another jail. Dying alone, but ironically, in the presence of two unknown officers. Michael, surrounded by the love and gratitude of supportive family and friends, present with him over many months and through every stage of his illness. If he bore anything alone, it was because of choice. John had none.

I sat beside John's bed, his handcuffed hand in mine. I talked to him, but no reply came. I prayed the Lord's Prayer, slowly, deliberately, finding myself pausing as I said, 'Forgive us our trespasses' – mine, and his. As I concluded, he clearly said 'Amen'.

To my words and prayers, Michael made no audible response. I was not to see either of them again.

> Lord, now lettest thou thy servant depart in
> peace, according to thy word.
>
> Luke 2:29 (BCP, *Nunc Dimittis*)

> *Lord, imprisoned by our fears,*
> *by our limitations, by our humanity,*
> *we seek you in all people*
> *and in all places.*
> *Be present with those who are dying,*
> *alone, or surrounded by love.*
> *Be present in the skills of those*
> *who care for the dying;*
> *in the care of all*
> *who work in our hospices.*
> *Be present in the hands*
> *of those who share love.*
> *Be present in those who*
> *minister there in your name,*
> *in word or deed,*
> *in silent presence.*

Information

The handcuffing of prisoners in hospital is, inevitably, an emotive issue. It highlights the tension between the provision of humane treatment of the sick and dying, and the need to protect the public from dangerous prisoners. Any use of restraint on a hospital escort or bed-watch has to be the subject of an individual risk assessment of the prisoner. This will consider the prisoner's index offence(s), length of sentence, previous convictions, current risk to the public, the prisoner's physical condition, and finally, their ability to escape – possibly with outside assistance. Any review of the initial risk assessment must clearly record any medical input from healthcare professionals with regard to the prisoner's current medical prognosis. Any use of restraints has to be proportionate and justifiable. If restraints are to be used, it is no longer permissible for a prisoner to be handcuffed to the bed. Handcuffing must only be to a member of the escorting staff.

Death

Just before eight o'clock in the morning, as I handed in my 'tally' in return for a set of keys, the Senior Officer in the Gate-house said, 'Can you contact Control, Chaplain?' The Control Room is the hub of the information network within the prison, laden with sophisticated machinery and banks of monitors showing pictures of all areas of the prison, coming from innumerable cameras. It is also the place where 'bad news' is received during the night.

In the room, accessible only after checks on my identity, I was handed the expected piece of paper, a Death of a Relative notification, with the first section carefully completed, the verification of details made through the hospital or local police, as necessary. Without such checks I could not inform a prisoner, given the number of 'hoax' calls which are received in the hope of distressing a prisoner, or getting a 'compassionate' visit, or even release on temporary licence (ROTL).

On this occasion I was satisfied and went to the wing where the prisoner was located and spoke with the officer on duty, seeking his insight into the likely reaction by the man, who was unknown to me. Simon was in a single cell, and with the agreement of the officer I decided to tell him in 'his own space'. The advice of uniformed staff is always crucial in such a decision, given the unpredictability and instability of some prisoners. There are times when it is necessary to give such bad news with the presence of an officer, and on neutral ground.

Knocking on the cell door and inserting my key at the same time, I was aware of the anxiety which always accompanies me at these times, no matter how often I have undertaken the task, one which everyone is very willing to pass to the chaplain!

As I opened the door and asked if I could come in, Simon's face registered 'the chaplain', early morning, and 'bad news', in an instant. I slipped the bolt, to prevent myself being locked in, and sat on the one chair in the cell, as Simon sat on the bed. I tried, with sensitivity, clarity and brevity to give Simon the news of the death of his grandmother. He allowed the tears to flow, unashamedly and unusually in this place where so many want to portray a hard-man image. We sat, the silence broken only by his tears and infrequent words. Sitting in openness, doing nothing but being present, is not easy. Sometimes it's possible here, sometimes it's not.

As time passed and the wing came to life outside the cell, Simon asked if he could attend the funeral, whenever it might be. In turn, I asked if she had ever acted *in loco parentis*. No, she had not. And so I explained that he must make application to the governor, but permission to attend a funeral is usually only given for a 'close' relative – a mother, father, sister, brother, wife, son, daughter, or a grandparent who had acted *in loco parentis*. Simon's disappointment was plain. I offered him the opportunity to come to the chapel at the time of the funeral, and for us to have some prayers together. Despite representations by the Chaplains to Prison Service Headquarters to have grand-parents included as 'close family', even when they have not acted *in loco parentis*, the situation remains largely unchanged. It is possible, with a full 'risk assessment', for Governors to use their discretion in this matter.

As expected, his application had been refused and we sat, side by side, with God, in front of a lighted candle in the chapel, otherwise alone, just a few days later. Using some of the same prayers that were being used in the crematorium at about the same moment, was helpful to him in his grief.

As we talked afterwards, he said he was glad he had not gone to the funeral, though he wanted to be there. The prospect of being handcuffed to two prison officers in front of his family and friends was not appealing. That afternoon, he had a visit from his parents.

> If there is no resurrection of the dead, then Christ has not been raised; and if Christ has not been raised, then our

proclamation has been in vain and your faith has been in vain.

1 Corinthians 15:13–14

God of all consolation,
grant to those who grieve
the spirit of faith and courage,
that they may have the strength
to meet the days to come
with steadfastness and patience,
not grieving without hope,
but trusting in your goodness;
through him who is the resurrection and the life,
Jesus Christ our Saviour.

From A New Zealand Prayer Book[18]

A few days later, I saw Jim, a 'lifer' who had just exercised one of the few controls which he had left over his own life, and had taken it. His broken body lay before me.

All our efforts to trace a relative or friend were to no avail.

In the cemetery, the undertaker's assistants lowered the coffin into the ground and withdrew to their car. I was left alone to say the funeral service, wanting to do so with dignity, for Jim's sake, yet uncertain as to why I should bother, and feeling guilty about such a thought going through my mind.

I knew that my role was representative, of the Church of which I was a member, of the Prison Service, of Jim's few friends in prison, of a community repulsed by his offences and who would not want reminding of his life. Yet I was deeply disappointed by my apparent lack of faith in the words of hope and resurrection, by my sense of isolation at a grave where even the undertaker's men seemed symbolically to reject Jim's corpse. Even in death there was no escape from the stigma of being 'a prisoner'.

I don't know who it was, but someone once said, 'To work in a prison you need an infinite capacity for disappointment.'

But this I call to mind, and therefore I have hope: the

steadfast love of the Lord never ceases, his mercies never
come to an end.

Lamentations 3:21–22

Lord, in disappointment
you give us hope,
in hope, love,
in love, your presence.
Enable us in honesty
to express our fear and anxiety,
our need to be restless
until we rest in you.
In your goodness
grant us wisdom and grace.

Victims

I received the invitation unexpectedly, and initially I thought it had come to me by mistake. Would I attend the launch of SAMM in East Anglia? SAMM, Support After Murder and Manslaughter, a national organisation dedicated to supporting and helping the families and friends of murder and manslaughter victims, were holding this very public launch in County Hall, also home to the Norfolk Constabulary HQ.

It was the first time I had been invited to any victim-support group, and I wondered why. After all, I was one of those charged with caring for the offender, not the victim. When I met John Davis, one of the people behind the launch, he spoke of some offenders as victims too. His realism, and pain, were evident. He and his wife Bernie had experienced the killing of their son, Jason, in January 1995 in Worcester. A young woman, also in the house at the time, had been seriously sexually abused.

After nine years of 'compartmentalising' my ministry in prison, I now came face to face with some of those who were at the receiving end of the deeds of some of those I cared for.

John and Bernie's eloquence and commitment to SAMM could not hide the depth of their grief; their continuing pain and anguish were a part of their physical presence. Bernie spoke of the choice which 'evil and wicked people have, but for the families of victims, there is no choice.'

Behind her, on a display board, were photographs of some of the people killed by murder or manslaughter in East Anglia in recent years. As she spoke I realised I knew more than one of the men responsible. The colour photograph of two beautiful children and their mother caused me particular emotion. I was regularly seeing the man who had killed them.

Never before had I faced victims, or their families, in this way.

Touched, deeply moved, and uncertain how to handle the feelings deep within me, I left, humbled. I could not help feeling that somehow I was 'guilty by association'.

There are many groups committed to helping prisoners, ex-prisoners and their families. Few exist to support victims or their families. One speaker spoke of 'those who belong to this exclusive club, that no one wants to join'.

A few years later, I received a letter from John and Bernie. John wrote:

> we succeeded in getting the prison to allow us to have a face-to-face meeting with the offender who killed our son. Bernie had always said that at some stage she would want to sit across the table from him to get some questions answered about that night in January 1995 and to let him know how much damage and hurt he had done to so many people.
>
> As you will appreciate, it took a tremendous amount out of us, but we did achieve what we set out to do. What no one could understand, is that Bernie was doing no more than Jason would have expected of her – and she felt the burden she had been carrying with her for four years lift off her shoulders on that cold December afternoon when we walked out of the prison.

A few months later they met one of the people who had received one of Jason's organs – his liver. It was, they said, 'very emotional, but so positive'. The man who received Jason's liver was older than John and Bernie, and he had lived in fear since the operation that they would resent that 'he had lived when young Jason had to die'. The meeting dispelled that fear for him, and he left with a new peace within himself.

SAMM aims to:

offer understanding and support to families and friends, who have been bereaved as a result of murder and manslaughter, through the mutual support of others who have experienced a similar tragedy;

raise public awareness about the effects of murder and manslaughter on families and friends;

take up issues of concern arising out of the effects of murder and manslaughter;

promote and support research into the effects of murder and manslaughter on society.

SAMM has a membership of 2000 people bereaved through murder and manslaughter. Sadly, membership grows weekly. Organisations such as SAMM and Victim Support provide enormous practical and emotional support for many distressed people.

> Meanwhile, standing near the cross of Jesus were his mother, and his mother's sister, Mary, the wife of Clopas, and Mary Magdalene.
>
> John 19:25

Christ the victim,
in your crucifixion
the innocent suffered.

Christ the victim,
in your pain
is our pain.

Christ the victim,
in your despair
is our despair.

Christ the victim,
in your confusion
is our confusion.

Christ the victim,
in your isolation
you felt forsaken
by the Father.

In our isolation,
help us to share such feelings.
In sharing, to be supported.
In being supported,
to be restored.

Jason's killer received a life sentence, and is imprisoned. So, too, are Jason's family.

Information
For further information visit:
www.samm.org.uk and www.victimsupport.org.uk

Questions arise

Days after the launch of the Support after Murder and Manslaughter Group, I sat in chapel trying to say morning prayer.

The endless round of activity within the prison – the demands, the uncertainty, the frustrations, the effort of listening, the expectation of speaking – were tiring and mentally draining. The man convicted of the manslaughter of his wife and the murder of their two children, and whose photographs I had seen at the SAMM launch, was in need of time and care, as were others.

As I sat trying to focus my thoughts on prayer, recurring questions ran through my mind: What am I doing in prison? What is the nature of ministry to the person who has committed such crimes? Why am I visiting this person? What can I do anyway? What do I have to say? Of what use can I be? How can I cope with what I hear? What is it that keeps me in this place?

Because it is here that I need God most. Here, that I recognise and acknowledge that need in a way that I have not done in my ministry outside. Here, where I have daily to seek him, and sometimes, to find him.

Alone in the chapel, with the hustle and bustle of 'A' Wing just metres away, with the noise of voices and the clanging of metal, I sat and tried, once again, to pray. I failed to do so, but I acknowledged my need, and ignored the written word before me.

As I sat, the words of a hymn came to my mind, words from 'I the Lord of sea and sky'. I read them and prayed them, especially holding onto 'I will hold your people in my heart'.

Acutely aware of the need for renewal of strength, vision and calling, I was further helped by the words, 'let the light of your love always shine in our hearts'.

God's love, not mine. I read the passage on which the hymn is based and left the chapel to see the new arrivals.

> Then I heard the voice of the Lord saying, 'Whom shall I send, and who will go for us ?'
> And I said, 'Here am I; send me.'
>
> Isaiah 6:8

> *Lord, in the depths*
> *you are there.*
> *In the questions*
> *you are present.*
> *In the uncertainty*
> *you are certain.*
> *In our weakness*
> *you are strength.*
> *In our inadequacy*
> *you are love.*
> *In our failing*
> *you are vision.*
> *Lord, let the light*
> *of your love*
> *be present with us,*
> *let your voice*
> *call us once again.*

The prayer of another chaplain, in a jail notorious throughout America, also reflected my mood. Pierre Raphael, then one of the chaplains in Riker's Island (a New York jail which at that time held 13,500 prisoners, and can hold up to 18,000), wrote 'The Chaplain's Prayer for Breath':

> *Lord, in the prison I will not survive nor will I progress unless my eyes find you and rest on you.*
> *Of course, I have the help of some of my friends, my sisters and brothers. We share a great deal, and not only our scars, our risks and our visions. All that is a very practical*

gift, not only useful but indispensable. It would be very naive to come here without friendships, complementary, unproblematic relationships that are simply normal. Lonesome cowboys belong on the prairie, not in the prison.

But, Lord, I need the certainty of your presence when I pace the corridors, enter the cells and receive, day after day, like a blow on the head, the evidence of evil and of a world in fragments.

I need to believe in you through all that is life in me, so as not to know the defeat of your absence, for everything here, all the blows, cries and tears, seem to scream of it. I need your presence minute by minute. I have tried so many times to tell my imprisoned friends that freedom, which is such a huge, corrosive dream when it batters itself against the shadows, can revive the dead, even here, when we choose once and for all to depend on you; when we decide quietly, practically, correctly, daily, to be familiar with your words, with your life; when we choose the means to seek you, to accept our waiting, without brutalizing anything of the precious gift, the nourishment that is offered to us.

Finally, when you are Master, Shepherd, Friend in our lives, one stage is finished. Another opens to us, like a new universe.

Every day, before going in, before passing through the bars, remind me to take the time necessary to mobilize joy.[19]

Wholeness and the therapeutic community

Grendon Prison is the only designated therapeutic prison in the country. It is a Category B Training Prison which has just over 200 prisoners, of whom 140 are serving life sentences. It is a place where it is expected that people will develop their potential, and where they will change. A critical part of the commitment of individuals to the therapeutic programme is motivation, and the acceptance by each person of himself, and the need to care for himself. This involves a quest for the truth about the self.

For those who have undergone therapy there has been a significant reduction in re-offending rates and these have been lower than in those who have not undergone therapy. Not all succeed, however, and a percentage of men return to 'normal' prisons without having completed the therapeutic process. No similar facility exists for women prisoners. A former Anglican chaplain reflects on what it means to be a Christian chaplain in this therapeutic community and on the need to seek wholeness.

Not many days go by without my having to think and pray about what it means to be a chaplain in a therapeutic community, or, because little or nothing is done without other Christian people in this place, what it means corporately to be the Christian presence in such a place. Many insights go into the quality of life we share together, and to which many professional disciplines contribute.

The Christian contribution is not particularly valued for itself. Many people think it to be irrelevant, outmoded, distracting or positively harmful. For a therapeutic community is little different from any other community outside in the range of belief systems which are represented in it by both staff and residents. Those who do seek to exercise their discipleship in such a place have to face many accusations, that they are using their faith as an escape from reality, that they are refusing to face up to their actions, that they are falsely relying on supposed other-worldly resources instead of seeking to order their own lives, that they substitute some idea of quick-fix forgiveness for a realistic exploration of their own responsibility for what they have done to others. We pay the price daily for the distortions and misunderstandings which abound about the kind of new life Christians enjoy as members of the Church of Jesus of Nazareth.

Retreat into the 'spiritual' will not do. That simply reinforces the idea that many non-believers have, that we are laying claim to be working in some special sphere which is quite different from the ordinary concerns of psychotherapy and which is certainly not subject to any of the tests of efficacy used by those with secular presuppositions.

What we have to do is to recognise areas which we have in common and stand firm on the differences.

All of us in a therapeutic community are looking for the truth about people, however painful it may be. We need to see ourselves as we are and not as we have taught ourselves to appear. There is no shortage of stories in the New Testament about those who are challenged to drop the masks and let their true selves be seen. The woman at the well, not surprisingly evasive about her marital history, and also indulging in theological games, is also a searcher for the truth and brings others to the source of that truth. The thief on the cross had a moment of disclosure which shows his real self, not just simply as a hopeless recidivist, but as one who is promised eternal life.

Life in a therapeutic community involves a search for the real person and not just the one whose persona has been overlaid by years of rejection and who, as a result, has learned to be someone different from themselves.

We are all interested in change. Some Christians might want to use the word 'conversion', but it would not help. What is the motivation which brings about real change in people? Can disgust at one's past life, a growing awareness of what one has done to victims and loved ones, a sense that one has been playing a part, a comparison of experience with others who have faced similar problems, some increase in self-esteem, an enhanced capacity to communicate – can these processes bring about change? Yes, thank God, for many they do. But for others that will not be enough. They will want to examine, to revisit some nagging questions about life's purpose; they will sense that human solutions are not all; that they have always had as a part of them a feeling for the God dimension, or they will find for the first time that they cannot make sense of themselves without it.

We are all interested in wholeness, although I find this word little used. Jesus' healing ministry illustrates again and again the inter-connection between the different aspects of ourselves. Our guilt feeds our worries; our worries can make us ill; our illnesses feed our anxieties; our anxieties make us demanding and impossible in our relationships; the breakdown in our relationships makes us more anxious; our anxiety can breed unreasonable and offending behaviour which feeds our guilt – and so, all too often, the whole dreary business goes on in a descending spiral of frustration which is all too familiar to anyone who works with those who have fallen foul of the law.

A healing ministry cuts through this vicious circle and introduces the possibility of newness and wholeness. 'Take up your bed and walk.' There is no need any longer to be dependent on the crutches and supports which have held back the disabled person from the right kind of independence and from being able to order his or her own life as a mature and responsible human being. Many interventions which can reverse the downward descent will come from the insights and processes of secular therapy, but finally, for Christians, wholeness comes only from the rediscovery of the image of God in that particular person through the work of the Lord.

'But so that you may know that the Son of Man has authority on earth to forgive sins' – he then said to the

paralytic – 'Stand up, take your bed and go to your home.'
Matthew 9:6

Lord God, thank you that you mediate healing to men and women in many ways and through many professional disciplines. Thank you for the search for the truth, the understanding of ourselves, the awareness of what we have done to others and the possibilities of living differently which can be learned in a therapeutic community. Help us with humility and integrity to live out that wholeness of life which alone comes from the healing touch of Christ and in the power and inspiration of his Spirit.

Absence

Nick was not an attender at chapel, or any chaplaincy activity, but we met frequently. Our first contact arose as a result of his being referred to me by a psychologist, a colleague within the prison. She was concerned about the enormous guilt carried by this young man. He had been in prison for a couple of years, serving 'life' for the murder of a young child.

Sigmund Freud said that people who feel guilt torment themselves for their bad behaviour without needing external judgement. Of the many people I have met in prison over many years, this was particularly true in Nick's case. Torment described his daily life. It was not physical, for he had been accepted by other prisoners. The anguish which he experienced was mental and spiritual. His torment was evident in his daily life, acknowledging the horror of his offence. It was hideous. He never sought to provide excuse, to plead any sort of miti-gating circumstance, but constantly wrestled with what it meant for him to be alive, and his victim dead.

Nick believed in God and over three years I tried to link his story with the greater story of God's pain. I could not.

Nick's belief in God was expressed through his sense of the absence of God in his life. Absence and presence are two aspects of the divine experience for many of us. Dietrich Bonhoeffer was imprisoned and executed for his beliefs during the Second World War. Whilst imprisoned he wrote: 'The God who is with us is the God who forsakes us (Mark 15:34) ... Before God and with God we live without God.'[20]

Nick was tormented by his guilt and by his feeling of God's absence, despite his belief. We tried to explore what it meant to experience the absence of that God.

R. S. Thomas, an Anglican priest and a poet of the last century, wrote passionately of the silence of God, of his absence:

It is this great absence
that is like a presence, that compels
me to address it without hope
of a reply. It is a room I enter
from which someone has just
gone, the vestibule for the arrival of one who has not yet
    come.

R. S. Thomas, 'The Absence'

For Nick, the resonance was acute.

God of presence,
help us to understand your absence.
Help us to understand
that in the absence
you call us
to know you.
We hold before you
our sense of being forsaken,
that through it we may acknowledge
that without you, we are without hope.

The ministry of reconciliation

We sat side by side in the small chapel in the Prison Health Centre. I was robed to symbolise my representative priestly role, or to hide my humanity, vulnerability and confusion over what I was doing.

A lighted candle was on the altar, representing the light of Christ in dark and broken lives.

Tom's life was badly broken. As were the lives of those who were his victims. The woman he loved, and the child they created and for whom, he said, there was no time for confession. Now, he wanted to take upon himself their sin, as well as to express his own.

I hear many 'confessions', but few in the formal setting usually associated with that word. Even in prison. Perhaps, especially in prison.

Falteringly, I began with some words from 1 John 1, associating myself with Tom: 'If we say that we have no sin, we deceive ourselves, and the truth is not in us. If we confess our sins, he who is faithful and just will forgive our sins and cleanse us from all unrighteousness.'

Tom had prepared himself well for this moment, when he would, in God's presence, make a humble confession of his sins. Hard as it was, he had taken care to think about the way he wanted to express his repentance. As I sat and listened, aware of our common humanity, I thought of the great cost involved in forgiveness – for the person confessing, God, and those called to embody it.

None the less, and despite all I have heard and read of people's offences, I was ill prepared for this catalogue of acts which seemed to distort what it means to be human. But Tom, I felt, was not simply seeking absolution for his sin. It was deeper and more significant than that, and later, in my reading

I began to understand what it was. An American Methodist and theologian, L. Gregory Jones, in his book, *Embodying Forgiveness*, writes:

> As such, a Christian account of forgiveness ought not simply or even primarily be focused on the absolution of guilt; rather, it ought to be focused on the reconciliation of brokenness, the restoration of communion – with God, with one another, and with the whole Creation.[21]

He tells us that forgiveness is a 'craft', which Christians need to learn to embody. A 'craft' rooted in a Trinitarian understanding of God.

Tom's confession was, for me, another stage in that continuous learning and understanding of God's love, and of trying to gain skill in the 'craft'. For Tom, perhaps, it was the beginning of reconciliation.

> Then I acknowledged my sin to you,
> and I did not hide my iniquity;
> I said, 'I will confess my transgressions to the Lord,'
> and you forgave the guilt of my sin.
>
> Psalm 32:5

> *Almighty and everlasting God,*
> *you hate nothing that you have made*
> *and forgive the sins of all those who are penitent:*
> *create and make in us new and contrite hearts,*
> *that we, worthily lamenting our sins*
> *and acknowledging our wretchedness,*
> *may receive from you, the God of all mercy,*
> *perfect remission and forgiveness;*
> *through Jesus Christ our Lord.*
> *Common Worship*, Collect for Ash Wednesday

Prisons Week

Prisons Week was started in England in 1975 (originally called Prisoners' Week), and Prisons Sunday is the third Sunday in November, with the week observed until the following Saturday.

It is an ecumenical observance supported by many churches throughout England, Wales and Scotland each year. Themes such as 'The Least of These', 'Worthless or Talented', and many others, are addressed over the course of the week.

The Prisons Week Committee is made up of prison chaplains, former prison chaplains, and other Christians working with prisoners and their families. The aim of the week is to encourage all Christians to focus their thoughts and prayers on prisoners, prisoners' families, victims of crime, prison staff, and all working in related areas. Increasingly the week is being marked by faiths other than Christianity, and by inter-faith observances.

> *Lord, you offer freedom to all people.*
> *We pray for all those who are in prison.*
> *Break the bonds of fear and isolation that exist.*
> *Support with Your love: prisoners, their families*
> *and friends, prison staff and all who care.*
> *Heal those who have been wounded by the activities*
> *of others, especially the victims of crime.*
> *Help us to forgive one another, to act justly,*
> *love mercy and walk humbly together with*
> *Christ in His strength and in His Spirit,*
> *now and every day.*

Prayer reproduced by kind permission
of the Prisons Week Committee (www.prisonsweek.org)

It is a week when many prisoners feel they are able to get involved in some of the events which take place. Ted is one such prisoner, and he wrote the following prayer for use during the week:

Heavenly Father, you see us for what we are:
men who are searching, and those who have found:
those driven by fear and those comforted by faith;
souls burdened by guilt and grief,
or lifted by love and companionship.

You know where we have come from:
cherished by a loving family and respected by our peers,
or from the fringes of society, unvalued and alone;
from lives of security and comfort, or from want and
  distress.

We have come before you in all our differences,
but united in our common desire to serve you in our daily
  lives.
Lord, captivate our souls and free us from sin;
surround us with your love and release us from loneliness.

We thank you for the prayers
and deliberations of Prisons Week:

Take me prisoner, Lord
And truly set me free;
Help me lay down my sword,
Then victorious shall I be.

Taking leave

A number of times I have been surprised by prisoners saying to me, 'After you left my cell,' or, 'When you left the wing, there was a different feeling for a time – a sense of peace.'

We need to listen to this sort of comment, not because it makes us feel good as chaplains, but because it contains a deep theological truth. It is right that our leaving is as good as our coming. For the way in which we leave can create a space for the work of the Spirit of God; for God to be present, and experienced, in some new way. It is right that there should be a difference when we have left. And that difference should encourage an intimacy with God, through his Spirit.

Some chaplains will always offer a prayer before leaving a cell, and through such prayer and presence the living God may be encountered.

> Nevertheless, I tell you the truth: it is to your advantage that I go away, for if I do not go away the Advocate will not come to you ...
>
> John 16:7

> *God our Father,*
> *as your Son prepared*
> *to take leave of his disciples,*
> *he promised the presence*
> *of your Spirit, the Advocate.*
> *May we encounter your*
> *Spirit of love*
> *and through him, your peace.*

The word across the prison world

Most prisons in England and Wales are fortunate in having a good relationship with the local branch of the Gideons. Operating internationally, this group, dedicated to spreading the word of God in the Bible, distributes millions of Bibles and New Testaments world-wide. Each year in the United Kingdom they are responsible for ensuring delivery to schools, hospitals and hotels. One little-known aspect of their work is in prison, where they supply thousands of New Testament & Psalms each year.

Stories abound about the value of the Gideons Bibles and New Testaments. I want to include two stories, linked together in a common thread, but separated by thousands of kilometres. The first is written by a former chaplain in Vancouver, Canada who ministered in 50 prisons in Canada, New Zealand and the USA during 50 years, and has regularly produced prayer material for those in prison. He has done so from a variety of faith perspectives. He writes:

Ben and I sat together on the side of his bed, in his cell. We had eaten supper together and now there was a time for fellowship. I sat holding Ben's leather-bound Bible, every book in it marked by a tab, page after page of verses underlined and with notes. Ben's Bible told the story of a man who had found God and in the process had found life.

Ben was doing two years, on the advice of a legal aid lawyer, for a crime he said he had not done. When he unexpectedly was sent to jail, the consequences were catastrophic. He lost his job and his family, and he felt there was no future, no hope, no justice.

He was reluctantly persuaded to attend chapel on his first Saturday in prison. He was oblivious to the whole service, but at its conclusion the chaplain handed him a New Testament.

On the return to his cell he threw it at the toilet. When nature next called he picked it up and read a verse of comfort on its foreleaf – 'I have set before you life and death, blessings and curses. Choose life.' In the moment it took to read that verse, the hurting, the hate, the hopelessness fell away and Ben said he felt the presence of God – a God of love who cares.

Ben read that New Testament from cover to cover, never finding those life-changing words from Deuteronomy 30:19. Months later he was put on the garbage detail. He wondered about being a Christian, but continued faithful. One day while emptying the garbage, a coverless book fell onto the ground. When Ben picked it up he found that it was a complete copy of the Bible. He hurriedly thumbed through it, finding that verse of salvation – 'I have set before you life and death, blessings and curses. Choose life …'

The Bible I held in my hand, was that precious book. He had bound it in brown leather and marked it prayerfully. With that miraculous book in my hand, he and I started giving thanks to our Father of blessing, and prayed:

> *Heavenly Father,*
> *you have set before us choices in life.*
> *Thank you for giving us eyes to see, ears to hear*
> *and hearts to respond to those choices.*
> *Help us to remain faithful to your Presence*
> *and to accept in joy your promises.*
> *Through Jesus Christ our Lord.*

*

Another chaplain recounts an occasion when he was making a visit to the chaplaincy at an English jail:

'You're the Vicar from Stafford, aren't you?'

The voice boomed across the landing bridge from what looked like an overgrown bramble-bush on the top of a man some six foot four inches tall. I had just stepped out of the chaplain's office to go to the chapel.

'Well, I was about six years ago,' I replied.

The prisoner reminded me that we had met in the Segregation Unit while he was confined there for police investigations.

'I used to listen for your footsteps every day,' he went on. He then dashed into his cell and emerged clutching a rather battered, but clearly much read, Gideon Testament.

'You gave me this. Your visits and this book were my lifeline then, and I still read it every day.'

For a second I felt proud, and then very humble as I remembered how often I would have been glad to give that visit a miss.

Other religious texts, such as the *Qu'ran* and the *Bhagavad Gita*, are just as important to adherents of those faiths. All are available through the chaplaincy, as are chaplains of those faiths.

> So shall my word be that goes out from my mouth;
> it shall not return to me empty,
> but it shall accomplish that which I purpose,
> and succeed in the thing for which I sent it.
>
> Isaiah 55:11

Lord, thy word abideth,
And our footsteps guideth:
Who its truth believeth
Light and joy receiveth.

O that we, discerning
Its most holy learning,
Lord, may love and fear thee,
Evermore be near thee.

Henry William Baker (1821–77)

Light behind bars

I first encountered the Prison Phoenix Trust when I was Anglican Chaplain of Wakefield Prison. At the time it was the largest maximum-security jail in Europe. It held 700 men, over half serving 'life', the other half in excess of four years.

A number of prisoners had read and been influenced by the book, We're all doing Time, *by Bo Lozoff.[22] Providing practical help and advice about meditation techniques, but not located in any particular 'religious' tradition, it was in steady demand. An invitation to the first Director of the Phoenix Trust, who distribute the book, led to a record number of long-term prisoners attending a discussion group on the Trust's work and on meditation techniques.*

The work of the Trust has grown, and there are now eight staff and ten volunteers to respond to the postbag from men, women, young offenders, juveniles, ex-offenders, and a small number of people in jails overseas. They write with great openness and insight into themselves, their crimes, and their distress.

In this piece, a former Director of the Trust writes about one of the 4000 prisoners with whom the Trust is in regular contact:

In some prisons, fear is almost palpable. The result is physical tension, both for inmates and prison officers. The Prison Phoenix Trust teaches some of the stretching exercises of yoga and other spiritual disciplines to help free the body from this bond, and to precede the actual meditation. We travel around the country giving workshops to staff and prisoners alike, and then prepare teachers to carry on the work. At the moment we support these teachers in over 90 prisons. When I came to the Trust four years ago, the first letter I opened was from an inmate called Paul in Norwich prison. He had just seen our newsletter, and submitted a poem called 'The Strip Cell' for us to print:

In the strip I sat
Humiliated, dejected, depressed.
It seems that no one cares. Do they?
Well, it seems not. Am I forgotten?
I hear a jangle of keys,
I bang, I shout, I swear,
It seems there's no one there. Is there?
At last someone comes; my saviour from this
hell – or not.
What do I want?
The screw shouts at me.
'Just a chat, Guv,' I say meekly.
'Not a chance, lad,' he grunts.
Is this real or an illusion?
Who knows or cares?

Over the years, I have come to know Paul rather well. He was born in Glasgow. His mother committed suicide when he was two years old, and the neglect and abuse he suffered at the hands of his alcoholic father led to his living in care in a series of homes, which inevitably ended in failure. He lived on the streets and learned a life of crime. His automatic response to any threatening situation was violence, and since the age of 14 he has been convicted of eight felonies. His behaviour inside prison had been equally destructive. He even attacked the prison visitor and broke his jaw. There is hardly a protest possible that he has not employed in an effort to vent the inner damage and pain.

One could only wonder whether meditation was having an effect on this young man. Then on his twenty-fourth birthday two years ago, he wrote a different sort of letter, reflective about his violent past and present, and sad to think that that might be all the future held for him too. 'I wish I could get my head straight,' he wrote. I encouraged therapy as an adjunct to his meditation, and eventually he came to Grendon, the country's only therapeutic prison.

From the start, his letters were different. He was speaking of

'Malcolm' and 'James' and 'Tim', explaining to me in the visitors' room later that they were the prison officers and governor. I remarked that it was good to learn that prison officers had names! Paul responded with a smile: 'And they call me Paul, too!'

Part of his healing was dependent on a reconciliation with the prison visitor who had been his victim. By the time he came to Grendon, his jaw had healed, and so had much of Paul's anger. It was a time of forgiveness and understanding for both, an experience Paul will not easily forget.

He is now in his last month in jail. He has had his first home leave of three days, visiting his girlfriend and setting up a room where he will live. He wants to work 'helping people'. He wrote that he reported back in prison 45 minutes ahead of time, and that the prison officers seemed very pleased with his progress. He ended his letter: 'I'm very pleased with myself too.' He has been given two names of people to whom he can go when he becomes confused or angry. I feel Paul now has a chance.

> But I have calmed and quieted my soul,
> like a weaned child with its mother;
> my soul is like the weaned child that is with me.
> O Israel, hope in the Lord from this time on and for ever
>   more.

Psalm 131:2–3

God, Father of us all,
you see the suffering of your children.
You see our loneliness, our sense of separation,
and our sometimes despair.
Help us to use these situations
to come to a realisation
that we are never alone,
that you are closer to us
than we are to ourselves,
and that in some mysterious way
we don't have to be anyone else,

or anywhere else, to find
a deep meaning and the possibility
of change in our lives.
For all of this lies hidden in our 'now' moment,
because we are your children,
and you are a caring Father.

Information
For more information visit: www.prisonphoenixtrust.org

Baptism

I have rarely baptised a prisoner, not primarily for theological reasons (though I have always encouraged short-term prisoners to wait until they become part of a worshipping community outside the prison), but rather, because there has been little demand! David Bosch, in his book Transforming Mission, *reminds us that 'People are never isolated individuals. They are social beings, who can never be separated from the network of relationships in which they exist. And the individual's conversion touches all these relationships.' Baptism must always be contextual and about transformation, not just satisfying people's needs.*

In this piece, submitted by a colleague (and to which I have added a prayer of my own and one from the Franciscan Service Book, Celebrating Common Prayer*), the joy and sense of new life contained within the baptism service is in stark contrast to the situation awaiting the prisoner on release, highlighting the words of Bosch.*

Christopher was a tall 16-year-old, with a mop of uncombed hair. He was polite, agreeable and wrote impressive letters with perfect spelling. His father had left his mother when he was two years old. His step-father threw him downstairs and broke his arm before he was five years old. Christopher lived in 26 different children's homes before he was imprisoned. He settled into the young offender institution quickly and enjoyed coming to chapel because he felt loved, and the chaplaincy volunteers from outside churches took an interest in him.

Two years into his sentence he asked me if he could be baptised. I prepared him, and some weeks before the service he asked if I could find his mother, and invite her to the service. He had not heard from her for over three years. Through the network of volunteers she was found almost a hundred miles away, invited to the service and collected on the day.

It was a great occasion. Christians from around the country had answered my request in the prayer-letter for cards of greeting, and there were over 80. The volunteers turned out in force, five clergy robed and took part, and many of his mates were present for a splendid service.

During the tea party that followed, Christopher's mother assured me that when he was discharged from prison just two days before Christmas, he would go and live with her. It was the best baptism present she could give him.

Seven days before his discharge Christopher received a letter from his mother in which she told of a new relationship with a man in the north-east of the country, and there would be no place for him after all.

> As many of you as were baptized into Christ have clothed yourself with Christ.
>
> Galatians 3:27

> *God of transformation,*
> *in baptism you confer*
> *new life in Christ.*
> *Grant that all who are*
> *baptised into his name*
> *may be enabled to keep*
> *the covenant they have made,*
> *and boldly confess him as Lord*
> *of life; and respond to the*
> *prompting of your Spirit.*

> *Almighty God,*
> *in our baptism you have consecrated us*
> *to be temples of your Holy Spirit:*
> *may we, whom you have counted worthy,*
> *nurture this gift of your indwelling Spirit*
> *with a lively faith,*

and worship you with upright lives;
through Jesus Christ our Lord.

Celebrating Common Prayer,
Collect for Epiphany 1

Restorative Justice

There is growing evidence that the Criminal Justice System is failing those most affected by crime. The victim's voice is often excluded, offenders are seldom helped to recognise the human cost of what they have done and the community fails to be reassured.

Restorative Justice (RJ) offers an alternative to the spiral of blame and retribution. It works from the premise that crimes are to be viewed less as violations against the state and more as violations against people. When seen through the restorative lens, the all-important question is not, 'Who is to blame?', but 'What can we do to help make things better for victims, the offender and the community?' Its priority, therefore, is to ensure that offenders are made fully aware of the damage they have caused and of their liability to repair that damage. Through a process of victim awareness/empathy programmes, offenders can be helped to repair the physical and emotional damage caused by crime. Victims and offenders are helped to view each other through different lenses. In meeting with offenders and telling their stories, a high percentage of victims testify to a greater sense of satisfaction than simply going through the courts.

HM Prison Service Chaplaincy is piloting 'SORI' (Supporting Offenders through Restoration Inside Prison) programmes in six prisons. SORI was devised and pioneered by a member of the chaplaincy team at HMP Cardiff in consultation with RJ practitioners. The programme, whilst sponsored by chaplaincy, works in partnership with various disciplines of the prison, including probation, reducing-offending teams, psychology, uniformed staff, and with Victim Support. They work together to ameliorate the harm done by crime for victims, offenders and the wider community.

Stuart was the archetypal drugs baron. He was top of the drugs pyramid for crack cocaine and heroin for the whole of South Wales, and ran ancillary businesses such as debt recovery and brothels. His family, upstanding members of a local church, and most of his friends, thought that Stuart's wealth came from his ownership of second-hand car dealerships and his role as manager of a local football club. He had played for a famous club as a young man.

The local police had been trying to catch up with Stuart for a decade, but he hid his criminal life well. When he was finally caught he was given a sentence of ten years.

He arrived at HMP Cardiff, stating that there were no victims to his crimes – he was just a businessman providing the community with a service – and that he had never met a drugs user anyway. He was only the wholesaler.

Stuart's father died soon after he came to prison, and through his contact with chaplaincy he was known as an intelligent and sensitive man. He was asked to help design the SORI course, and if he would be part of the first pilot run of the course with offenders.

Stuart agreed, but kept on repeating that whilst he'd help, he had no victims. One of the pivotal exercises of SORI involves a whole-group role play where offenders and tutors take on the roles of all the victims affected by a crime. Stuart volunteered his crime – just to be awkward – and it was suggested that his victims, for the sake of argument, could be his family members, who also ended up serving his sentence.

Participants took turns imagining how his family members might have felt: his bereaved mother coping with her damaged reputation following all the publicity; or his daughters, whose businesses had been funded, apparently, from 'dirty' money.

Through the process he began to realise with deep emotion that he did, in fact, have thousands of victims. With others on the course, he made a public apology. He also listened to drug takers talk of their losses and anger. He volunteered to work on the prison's detox wing where some of the users of his own drugs were located. He became a Samaritans Listener (see

'Listeners', p. 150), offering support for other offenders. On moving through the prison system to a 'D' Category prison, he volunteered to work with the police. In partnership with them, he gave talks in schools, seeking to deter young people from using drugs or getting involved in crime. He later got a job in the local Citizens' Advice Bureau, offering free business advice.

He continues to work with victims and offenders, promoting Restorative Justice, and has told his family the full facts of his offending, with complete honesty.

> *And what does the Lord require of you*
> *but to do justice, and to love kindness,*
> *and to walk humbly with your God.*

Micah 6:8

> Restore us, O God;
> let your face shine, that we may be saved.

Psalm 80:3

> *God of healing,*
> *you have called us to*
> *'do justice and love mercy';*
> *to heal the hurt,*
> *to mend the broken*
> *relationships of our lives.*
> *Fill us with the hope*
> *which reflects your*
> *grace and love;*
> *which seeks to repair the harm*
> *we have caused,*
> *and to restore us*
> *in your peace and salvation.*

PRISON STAFF

Called together

Historically, a Church of England chaplain has been appointed as 'The Chaplain' to a prison establishment. This is an anachronism and is seen, by some, as an affront to ecumenical understanding and inter-faith co-operation. Fraught with potential difficulties, it has, all too often, led to ministry being seen as the responsibility of one person. Every prison has a Roman Catholic and a Methodist Chaplain, though strictly within the understanding of the Prison Act 1952, they should be referred to as 'prison ministers', along with representatives of other Christian and world faiths. Such a pejorative expression, however, simply devalues the contribution of ministers of all faith-traditions, and the concept and understanding of ministry as a whole. Since 2003, and with the agreement of the Chaplaincy Council, the title of Chaplain has been applied to the representatives of most of the faiths in the prison system. The Chaplaincy Council is a multi-faith body that oversees the work of chaplaincy, and contributes to prison policy.

Henri Nouwen, in his book, *In the Name of Jesus*, explores the future of Christian leadership. He uses the analogy of ministers as failed tight-rope walkers who have discovered that they do not have the power to draw thousands of people; that they do not make many conversions; that they do not have the talent to create beautiful liturgies; that they are not as popular with the youth, the young adults, or the elderly as they had hoped; and that they are not able to respond to the needs of their people as expected. Despite this, many in ministry feel they should be able to do it all and to do it successfully. The rampant individualism which is so much a part of our competitive society is not alien to the Church, or the Chaplaincy.

Shortly before he died, Henri Nouwen wrote: 'We have been called to be fruitful – not successful, not productive, not accomplished. Success comes from strength, stress, and human effort. Fruitfulness comes from vulnerability and the admission of our own weakness.'

Such an understanding has had a profound influence on the way in which I have sought to exercise my ministry in prison, and I have been privileged to share that ministry with others who think in a similar way. It seems from the Gospels, that Jesus saw ministry as more than individualism. In Mark 6:7, where he sends the twelve out in pairs, there may be the grounds for a collaborative approach to ministry, with the implication that we cannot bring the 'good news' on our own. Throughout the years I have been part of a number of ministry teams, including at Chaplaincy Headquarters, I have seen the radical difference which ministry as part of a Team can make. We recognise that it is better for us, and at times easier, to pray together, rather than separately; that it is easier to share the spiritual task; that it helps to share the pain as well as the joy, and that it produces a challenge. Through ministry together, it is easier for others to recognise and accept that we do not come in our own name, but in the name of the Lord who calls us.

In the words of Mother Julian of Norwich, 'If I look at myself, I am nothing. But if I look at us all I am hopeful; for I see the unity of love among all my fellow Christians. In this unity lies our salvation.' Increasingly, with an inclusive, multi-faith approach to our ministry, Buddhists, Christians, Hindus, Jews, Muslims, Sikhs, and others, are sharing in the responsibility of caring for those in prison. Individually, we can do much; together, we can do even more.

> I ask not only on behalf of these, but also on behalf of those who will believe in me through their word, that they may all be one. As you, Father, are in me and I am in you, may they also be in us …
>
> John 17:20–21

God our Father,
you have called us to be your pilgrim people.

Through the work of your Holy Spirit
draw us ever closer to you and to one another.
Together may we pray and worship,
together may we work and rest,
together share our sorrows and our joys.
As we travel onwards
towards the unity for which Christ prayed,
show us the way
and give us the grace and the courage to follow it.

Information

The prayer above is adapted from one used in the Week of Prayer for Christian Unity material, and published with the permission of the Council of Churches for Britain and Ireland (formerly the British Council of Churches).

Living faith traditions

It was Ramadan, the month during which Muslims fast from sunrise to sunset. During that time I was frequently in the prison at sunset, and the Imam invited me to 'break-fast' with him. Together, we shared, in the presence of God, sometimes in silence, sometimes in dialogue, always with respect for each other's faith tradition. Shortly before I left that prison he invited me to his home for a meal. I was the first non-Muslim person to enter his home and to eat with him during his adult life.

The Sikh Chaplain regularly made me welcome at the *langar* (which literally means 'the common kitchen') to share in the food served after worship in the *Gurdwara* (Temple). The Gurdwara in the prison was a designated multi-faith room.

The Rabbi was always keen to discuss common issues relating to theology. The Buddhist Chaplain taught meditation techniques to some long-term prisoners, and his personal 'sense of peace' was palpable, and appreciated by all he met.

So many different people of living faith traditions are represented, and contribute to the life of so many prisoners and staff; to our understanding of God, and the richness of cultural and religious diversity in the spiritual aridness of the penal system.

It has been a privilege to encounter such people, to stand with them, to learn from them, and to reflect on what it means to be a Christian in dialogue with those whose faith is also 'living', and whose call to ministry brings them into prison.

My own understanding of faith and my relationship with God has benefited from being exposed to the faith and understanding of these people and their traditions. I have come to appreciate what David Bosch describes as the 'abiding paradox of asserting both ultimate commitment to one's own religion and genuine openness to another's'.

I am the God of your Father, the God of Abraham, the God of Isaac, and the God of Jacob …

Exodus 3:6

God of Abraham, Isaac and Jacob,
we give you thanks
for the richness and
diversity of faith.
With all your people
we open ourselves
to your living Spirit.
Enrich us with the ability
to encounter and to share;
that we may deepen
our understanding of your
presence, your love
and your grace,
in those made
in your image.

[Note: Imams are now referred to as Muslim chaplains.]

Busyness

Prisons are incredibly busy places. Local prisons, where people are received from the Courts (Magistrates, County and High), see thousands of receptions and discharges every day. Throughout the prisons in England and Wales there is constant movement of prisoners. All day people are moving from one place to another, to workshops, to court, to education, to groups, to be interviewed, to see a solicitor, to see a visitor. Meetings of one sort or another are taking place, prisoners are being reviewed, suicide prevention strategy is being planned, budget cuts and their implications are being faced. Prisoners are seeking attention, from prison officers, governors, teachers, probation officers, chaplains.

There is constant noise, and my office, adjacent to some telephones and to the reception area, is often filled with the sound of abusive language, as angry words are flung at relatives or friends, the police, or contracted staff bringing men to, or taking them from the prison. The noise is penetrative.

In the midst of this, at times, frantic environment, those who minister in prison may be easily tempted into 'justification by busyness'. The immediacy of ministry in prison makes demands which create an illusion for our busyness, our usefulness, our indispensability. Within the safe walls, the security of our busyness, the demands of our role, the self is often denied, and God too.

We need to be confident enough to step out of the security and safety of our role as chaplains, with our prescribed ways of thinking, subtly influenced by prisoners, staff, government policy, the Church, faith communities. Only then can we be truly creative, prophetic, concerned with wholeness. But the demands are huge: time for prisoners, staff, meetings, administration, the wider Church, our faith community. In the midst of this busyness we need space to acknowledge our basic lack of fulfilment, when we allow the Spirit to engage and challenge us.

'God is the still point at the centre,' wrote Mother Julian of Norwich. Privileged, as I was, to celebrate the Eucharist in her 'cell' in St Julian's Church in Norwich over many months, I became increasingly aware of the need to centre my life on God. Perhaps a start would be to look at the diary, to create time to be with God as readily as we create time for people or routine administration.

Be still, and know that I am God!

Psalm 46:10

Almighty God,
you have made us for yourself,
and our hearts are restless
till they find their rest in you:
Pour your love into our hearts and draw us to yourself,
and so bring us at last to your heavenly city
where we shall see you face to face;
through Jesus Christ our Lord.

Common Worship,
Collect for the 17th Sunday after Trinity

Living with risk

All who work in prison are at risk of physical, psychological or emotional harm. Staff face daily encounters with difficult and unpredictable people. Constant vigilance is necessary, but risks have to be taken as part of each working day, every encounter. A former colleague tells her story, and concludes it with a prayer:

When I was working as a Probation Officer I was responsible for 70 prisoners on one wing of the prison. Many were serving life sentences, often with very lengthy tariffs, or waiting for their tariff to be set. The offences they had committed had caused death or very serious harm to the victims. This in turn had often had a devastating affect on the victim's families. We read daily in the press the details of these types of offences.

As a Probation Officer the requirements of my job in the prison were offender focused and included preparation for, and delivery of, offending-behaviour programmes, participation in sentence planning, framing of risk assessments, development of release plans with outside Probation Staff and other relevant agencies. I worked closely with prison staff who themselves had needs and anxieties caused by the nature of the jobs they held. Sometimes I had to see families when they were visiting – this helped me to realise that offenders' families are frequently the unseen victims of the offences committed.

One of the requirements was that I made contact with each prisoner as he came on to the wing – from another prison or from another wing of our prison. In that way I tried to have personal knowledge of all those I was working with.

I was aware that there was a new prisoner on the wing who I had not seen and I was on the point of making an appointment to see him. Then, at a daily 'surgery' (when we saw prisoners to deal with any immediate needs), he came into my office – a converted cell – as if to ask me a question. I felt relieved that I had been saved the task of setting up an appointment. It did not turn out like that. Within seconds of entering the 'office' he had launched a violent attack on me and I was only saved when my screams were heard.

The days that followed, when I was coming to terms with what had happened, were characterised by excessive press interest – not because of me, but because of the prisoner who had perpetrated the offence – he is notorious and had attracted press interest ever since his arrest. Hate mail from other prisoners followed the attack, causing the police and prison more intelligence and preventative work.

The incident had some strange legacies. To this day, when a service I am attending includes the hymn 'To God be the Glory', I have to cover up my emotional reaction when we sing the line, 'The vilest offender who truly believes, That moment from Jesus a pardon receives.' I did not think he, or some others, deserved the privilege of forgiveness, nor could they manage the responsibility that forgiveness requires of us.

When some of the strongest feelings about the attack on me had subsided, I wanted to face him and ask him why he had done it. I suppose I was acting in my professional role, wanting to reduce further offending by seeing what the causes were. I didn't see him – the professional assessment was that it would not effect any change in his behaviour or in his risk of future harm or re-offending. One of the chaplains did see him to ask him the questions I had wanted to. Her assessment was that there was no change in his situation or attitudes, and that she would be more concerned for my situation if I were to pursue that course of action.

So what about forgiveness? Is he repentant? I do not know. That is for others to assess. He is serving a life sentence and the sentence-planning and risk-assessment process will be completed by all agencies involved long before a release plan can be put in place.

What I do know is that I was supported by so many colleagues and friends that I felt that God was there upholding me. Indeed, I have made new friends as a result. I have also learned how it feels to be a victim and know that it is an insight I can bring to my own work that was not possible before.

Some prisoners tell me that they will never re-offend. They may not have apologised, or in Christian terms, 'repented', but they want to lead a crime-free life. Does God forgive them? It is a question that has been asked by many theologians and chaplains and will continue to be asked long after my lifetime. I hope the debate does continue because I am dedicated to ensuring that offenders have the opportunities for changed lives. If those changes include involvement with a faith group, then that must be included in the plans that are made for eventual release. Both professionally and in the context of faith situations, I am insistent that offenders understand that such a commitment requires extra responsibilities and that members of the faith groups understand risk, and the need for protection of their congregations.

I am a survivor and still work as a Probation Officer. I continue to hope that there were lessons for us all to learn from the incident and that we have the will to continue that learning.

> We are afflicted in every way, but not crushed; perplexed, but not driven to despair; persecuted, but not forsaken; struck down, but not destroyed; always carrying in the body the death of Jesus, so that the life of Jesus may also be visible in our bodies.
>
> 2 Corinthians 4:8–10

> *Give us true repentance;*
> *forgive us our sins of negligence and ignorance,*
> *and our deliberate sins;*
> *and grant us the grace of your Holy Spirit*
> *to amend our lives according to your holy word.*

The man tried for this attack was found not guilty of attempted murder, but guilty of false imprisonment. Already serving four life sentences, he was given an eight-year sentence to run concurrently with his existing terms.

Prison officers

It is not uncommon to hear people, and the media, refer to prison 'warders' – sometimes in a pejorative way. The term 'warder' was last used officially in 1921. The term used since that time is 'officer', and this is more usually 'main grade' or 'discipline' officer.

The use of the word 'discipline' is interesting, given its etymological links. The root is the same as that used in the word 'disciple' and is about learning. It has at its very heart a connection to hope, linking as it does to the future, not to the past. The current recruitment brochure for prison staff states: 'Prison work is not for the fainthearted: it requires imagination, humanity, optimism and courage.' Optimism, learning and hope all link together in the daily life of those who work in our prisons, in any capacity, but they are especially needed by the men and women who 'walk the landings', engaging with prisoners daily. Some 27,000 of the 51,000 staff employed in the Prison Service are officers. All of them receive two months' training, which includes a six-week residential course at the Prison Service College, or, for those with primary-care responsibilities, training at one of the 12 local POELT (Prison Officer Entry Level Training) delivery venues.

To prepare for prison life, they are exposed to a wide range of subjects from racial awareness and inter-personal skills, to search techniques. They need them all. As Viv, a recently appointed officer, says, 'It can be unpredictable unlocking the cell of a man who has been locked up for over 12 hours; stressful dealing with the demands of some who are in prison for their inability to curb their demands; tiring being constantly vigilant, being aware of what is happening, who is speaking to whom, who is manipulating, bullying, dealing; conscious of the physical threat which underlies so much of prison life.'

The success of the Prison Service is that discipline officers, and others, go on doing such a good job with prisoners, but prison is a hard place to be. Viv recognises this: 'I can't believe I can make much of a difference; so many prisoners are manipulative, dishonest, trying to use me, and yet they have potential to be something different, which needs developing.' Many staff find it hard to leave the job at the gate when they go home. 'I find it hard to get things and people out of my head,' she says.

Frustration can also creep in, particularly in a local prison where prisoners constantly come and go, some staying for very short periods of time, others for many months. Viv acknowledges the difficulty of doing anything significant with people in so short a time, yet, as a Christian, she feels she can utilise even the briefest of opportunities to affirm and value many of those with whom she meets. 'Most of the time it's an interesting, but very different job. There are times when it's boring and threatening, but it can be rewarding, just occasionally. Before I started to work here I had a neutral attitude to prisons, now I have a passion for them and believe I'm doing something worthwhile. I just want people outside to know what's happening inside.'

> *Lord, it's a hard place to be,*
> *an uncomfortable place*
> *a frustrating place*
> *a stressful place.*
> *A place where encounters are unpredictable,*
> *not always what they seem*
> *and often surprising.*
> *We give you thanks*
> *for the dedication*
> *and care of staff*
> *as they serve our prisons.*
> *We ask for the gifts of*
> *optimism, patience, and hope*
> *that we may do*
> *something of your will.*

Governors

Under the Prison Act, 1952, every prison must have a Governor, a chaplain, and 'other such officers as may be necessary'. In the current difficult economic climate, with increasing emphasis on utilising business and organisational theory and concepts, there has been a sea-change in the way in which the role of the Governor is perceived. The man, or woman, entrusted with responsibility for the everyday running of a prison must now combine an array of abilities ranging from management expertise to entrepreneurial flair, whilst managing substantial budgets in the face of 3 per cent cuts, year on year for at least three years, and an increasing number of people in prison. It calls for considerable skill and personal resource.

Increasing devolution of responsibility to Governors and Senior Managers, from a diminishing number of people at Headquarters, has led to greater autonomy and to some governors being effectively 'Managing Directors' of medium-sized companies. For even a medium-sized prison will have a budget of some £15 million, and many have considerably larger budgets.

Set against an uncertain political background, and with the public understanding of the purposes of imprisonment being narrowly defined, governors have to juggle the often conflicting demands of security; the increasing lack of accommodation for an increasing number of people; reduced resources – financial and in personnel terms; raised expectations from prisoners in areas such as work, time out of cell, visits; and the potential risk of disorder as an expression of dissatisfaction, whilst trying to provide solutions which are in keeping with concepts of decency, humanity and justice.

Such demands may contribute to the need for a debate

about the purpose of imprisonment and about policies which should be in the best interests of victims, potential victims, offenders and their families. It must be of concern to many people that the philosophical basis on which the prison system should be based, needs rethinking.

Governors have to 'prioritise' the relative merits of disparate needs and benefits – weighing, for example, education and probation provision against security improvements or interventions or programmes designed to change people's behaviour. They are often 'between a rock and a hard place'. But their work is crucial to the delivery of the criminal justice system, to the lives of prisoners and staff.

Lord,
we hold in your presence
all who are called to be
governors in the Prison Service.
We pray that they may have the gifts
which are necessary to encourage
those who live and work
in prisons to achieve their potential;
to manage conflicting demands,
and to put the needs of individuals
at the heart of their work,
through justice and humanity.

In times of despair
give them hope;
in times of anxiety
give them strength;
in times of despondency
give them perseverance;
in all life, give them vision.

Education

Four inter-related short stories provide a glimpse into the world of prison education. Creatively crafted, they reflect the imagination and care of the teacher who wrote them. The writer has an infinite capacity to care for the marginalised, to seek out their inherent potential and to stand alongside them through their experiences. Each story is based on someone he has known. A Christian, his faith is reflected in his ability to be creative in every context – even, as we hear, in the midst of cut-backs and a diminution of the important work done in this field. After the four stories, I have added a prayer.

Wayne

114 admitted offences, fourth custodial sentence. Father and older brother convicted and currently serving sentences.

> For everything created by God is good, and nothing is to be rejected.
>
> 1 Timothy 4:4

'We did numeracy today. That's sums, really, but if you're thick, like me, you don't do maths, you do numeracy. The bloke teaching us was wearing the same shoes he had the last time I was in, doing a two for commercials. Sad shoes, I'm telling you. Couldn't be bothered doing the work, so I had a go at him. Told him I was thick and always had been – they told me so at school – and always would be. Thinking does my head in. He just smiled. Not laughing at me, like, just friendly. Told me I wasn't thick at all. Just lacked confidence, he said. Maybe I was scared of thinking, scared of thinking things through, he said. Told him straight, I did. Not lacking in confidence, was I, four floors up on the roof of the warehouse and coppers' dogs waiting for

me down below! He nodded, saying that he wouldn't like to be
in my shoes. So how much do you get for teaching us lot then,
I asked. Enough, he said. Not enough for a decent pair of shoes,
I laughed, pointing down at his manky Hush Puppies.
Wouldn't like to be in your shoes. Everybody laughed at him.
Told him I always wore best Italian leather on the out. I make a
couple of hundred an hour doing over warehouses. He wasn't
impressed. Said that wasn't much. Got angry at that – so I had
a right go at him and we all gave him some stick but he just
wrote it up. Wrote my 300 quid with his coloured pen. Then he
asked how much bird I got. Told him. He wrote up my time,
then started to do this sum – nice and slow so I didn't feel
stupid and could keep up. We worked out how many working
days there were in my sentence. Then we divided the bung I
made by the length of time I got. Came out at less than two
quid a day. Got a hell of a shock, seeing it up there in blue and
white. Two quid a lousy day. Scared me. Makes you think,
though, dunnit?'

> Before that sudden journey none is wiser in thought than
> he needs to be, in considering, before his departure, what
> will be adjudged to his soul, of good or evil, after his
> death-day.
>
> Bede's Death Song (AD 735)

Robert
Homeless, single and inadequate – drifting into petty crime
and heavy drinking.

> Full of doubt I stand,
> Whether I should repent me now of sin
> By me done and occasioned, or rejoice
> Much more that much more good thereof shall spring,
> To God more glory, more good-will to men
> From God, and over wrath grace shall abound.
>
> John Milton, *Paradise Lost*, Book XII.473–8

'Come on, come on. Get them open. I hate this bit, waiting for them to open the gates. Over a hundred years old, these gates. CCTV cameras are new. Just think, on the other side, when I get through, there'll be friends, familiar faces. I'll be sorted. Loads to do. Lots to catch up on. Who's doing what. All the gossip. All the news. I always get this buzz at the gate.

'Come on, come on. What's the hold-up? Oh, it's the screws coming back from the Mess. Did a spell in the Mess on the fryers. That little woman from education said I did her chips just the way she likes them. Always thanked me, proper like. Got me roped in on a Food Hygiene course. Did it. Got the certificate. Then she mugged me again, got me to do a Health and Safety course. Got that too. She didn't talk much, but really listened. That's how I ended up going to the AA group and started to be honest about my drinking. Kept on at me, though. So I started to go to evening classes. Didn't know I was good at art. And the history was interesting, too. She said I should go down to the college when I got out and carry on. Me? At college? I laughed. She just nodded and gave me the name and phone number of a teacher she knows there.

'Come on, come on. Open these gates. I'm buzzing. Through those gates and I'll be back with people who care, people who take the time to get to know me. That little woman from education always called me by my first name. Six hundred of us coming and going and she always remembered my first name. All the teachers the same. Great, things are moving. Here we go. Open, sesame. They're closing the gates behind me. I'm back – back in a world where there's food, a welcome and plenty to do, friends and people who know your name.

'Can't wait to get through Reception. Get my kit and onto the landings. Might even get the same old cell. I didn't make it down to the college – this time. But I'll apply to get onto classes. Finish that picture of the barn owl. Back inside. Just like coming home.'

With such certainty ascended He,
The Son of Man who deigned Himself to be:

That when we lifted out of sleep, there was
Life with its dark – and love above the law.

> Denis Devlin, *Ascension*

John

Risk-taking entrepreneur. Imports fine wines. Sentenced for five specimen charges of VAT evasion.

Cast thy care upon the Lord,
And he shall nourish thee Himself.
When I cried to the Lord,
He heard my cry.

> Traditional verse, after Thomas à Kempis

'At public school they said – after this, one shall be equal to anything one might encounter in later life. They were not quite right. The bullyboys and the food in here would be no match for the miseries of the Lower Fifth. Still, stiff upper lip. That's my motto. The family motto is longer, and in Latin, but amounts to the same thing. Of course, I refused to have absolutely anything to do with my people when I came into prison. Right thing to do. Frightful shame and all that. Simply couldn't face the parents. No visits. No letters. Then that lady from education came along to see me – just like Matron used to see the young boarders in their first week away from home. Decent enough type, but I told her I spoke four languages and had enough of the classics to last me a lifetime. Had her down as a sort of WRVS wallah, meals-on-wheels for the mind. We talked, and she advised me to keep in touch with my family. Visits were important, she stressed. Keep in touch with the loved ones. No need on my part, I told her. For their sake, she replied. Thought about it. Dammit, she was right. Wrote to them that night.

'Rather afraid I've been a bit of a fool all round. Had a chat with that education lady. She asked me how was my Italian. Then asked me if I had any Albanian. Wonder what the old trout's up to. Asked her for a book on cheese. Said she'd oblige.

Sure enough, she came the next day. Exactly what I wanted, together with a guide to setting up in business. Book-keeping and simple accountancy. Useful stuff. Signed up for a course they run for the self-employed. Pity they didn't teach me that years ago. I believe we will cover VAT too. Ironic, really. I can quote yards of Horace but go into a blue funk with figures and accounts. She said she'd introduce me to software packages for spreadsheets and stock control. Never had patience for all that nonsense before. Know better now. I'll be steering clear of fine wines next time round, though. Go for continental cheeses. Wonder if HM Revenue & Customs whack excise on Emmenthal. I'll ask that lady from education. She's bound to know.

'The parents are coming tomorrow. I'm so glad. I do hope the pater doesn't do his Sandhurst stunt and inspect the prison officers as he walks in.'

As, O God, we believe and hope for the good things of eternity, grant that we may so use the transitory miseries of this life as to obtain the permanent felicity of the next.
                                                    Thomas à Kempis

The Teacher

'It's going to be tricky providing for that Albanian deportee. Still, we manage it with the Ethiopians, the Romanians and those four Turkish inmates up on the Threes landing. I'll see the landing officer and ask for a cell change before bang-up. Get him in with John. They both have a little Italian between them. Well, it's a start. Oh, and I mustn't forget that book on cheese. So glad he made it through the first week. Often his type stoically fall on their swords. He's off the at-risk list, and has signed up for the business skills course. I believe he's expecting a visit soon. His mother took it all very badly, I gather.

'Wayne is a bright young man. I wonder where he'd be now if he'd had John's chances. Too soon to suggest he does a numeracy exam, I think, but he should eventually. Next month, perhaps. For so many of them it's a fear of failure, but for Wayne it's fear of success. Proven, measured intelligence is an uncomfortable burden for those whose plea is always ignorance. Exposes them to a greater sense of responsibility. Pity so many have to do the painful parts of growing up inside prison.

'Robert is back. Seemed almost relieved to be back here. Dreadful fact is that this is his home. His whole way of life built around the overestimated comforts of prison.

'The wing is down after the suicide last week. I've proposed a strategy of seeing all prisoners for an informal briefing and settling-in session every morning. Screen out the disturbed and the vulnerable, but everything costs and the sniffer dogs and the CCTV eat into the budget. Cutting the pencils in half should stretch our capital a little further, but it won't bring back the two music teachers.

'Last month's exam results were excellent – so rewarding and motivating for the men here. They have such low expectations, such low self-esteem. As much failed by early learning experiences as failing within them, I'm sure. We don't have the luxury of a hidden curriculum here, we just make sure we deliver the provision with extra support, care and love. Trouble is, the men initially find this more difficult to grasp than the percentages, gerunds and trigonometry. Harder for them to learn that they merit and need such care.'

> *Domine non sum dignus.*
> (Lord, I am not worthy)

*

Education in prisons contributes positively to the dynamic security, safety and care of prisoners. It plays a key role in addressing their offending behaviour; challenging their low self-esteem; assessing their untapped potential and assisting them to prepare for the challenges and opportunities on their release. But almost 50 per cent of prisoners are at, or below, the level expected for an 11-year-old in reading, 65 per cent in numeracy, and 82 per cent in writing. And half of all prisoners do not have the skills required by 96 per cent of jobs. Only 1 in 5 are able to complete a job application form. Prison Service targets for the number of prisoners achieving different skills qualifications are very high, with 42,500 basic skills awards, and 146,053 key work skill awards, in 2005/6. Yet Home Office research has shown that improvements in literacy and numeracy were not significantly related to prisoners' chances of finding employment or re-offending after release. Factors such as links with previous employers and family contacts were more strongly related to employment outcomes. (See www.prison reformtrust.org.uk)

As is clear from the above narratives, education staff can play a crucial and enabling role in the life of some prisoners, helping to bring about change. Education can provide an environment in which there can be a real sense of achievement, of progress, of moving forward, in a place where life, and time, seem to stand still for so many.

> Now when Jesus had finished saying these things, the crowds were astounded at his teaching, for he taught them as one having authority, and not as their scribes.
>
> Matthew 7:28–29

Christ the Teacher,
in your presence the people were
'astounded' at your teaching.

We give you thanks
for those who are
called to be teachers,
to exercise the creativity
which opens minds and hearts
to other perspectives,
other ways.

Be present through

their skills of mind and imagination,
that they may inspire and encourage,
through vision and freshness of thought,
those with whom they sit.

Bless and nurture their contribution
to truth, love, and the development of potential,
and in so doing, may lives be transformed.

CONNECTED GROUPS

The Independent Monitoring Board

A routine telephone call, regular, but not frequent: 'Could you see John Mills on "B" Wing? He doesn't know what to do about his child and he needs someone to talk to about the situation.'

Pat is a member of the Independent Monitoring Board (IMB), a group of about 13 voluntary lay members, two of whom must be magistrates, and appointed to every prison, including those in the contracted-out sector, and all young offender institutions in the country.

Members are appointed by the Secretary of State and have an important role in monitoring the fair treatment of prisoners on his/her behalf, and as representatives of the wider public, in whose communities prisons are placed and in whose name prisons are run.

The principle of independent inspection of prisons in this country dates to Tudor times, and members of the IMB have a right of access to any part of a prison, at any time. The Board is expected to raise matters of concern with the prison governor, or the director/controller in a privately managed prison, or with the Regional Manager, Custodial Sentences, responsible for that prison. If necessary, the matter may be taken to the Secretary of State.

Board members are expected to hear any complaint made by a prisoner, satisfy themselves as to the state of the prison premises, the running of the prison and the treatment of prisoners. In addition, they must inquire into and report on any matter of concern which the Secretary of State asks them to investigate; bring to the attention of the governor any issue they consider important; inform the Secretary of State of any abuse which may come to their attention.

Whilst all of this might seem quite far removed from the everyday concerns of prisoners, Board members also have to inspect the food of prisoners at frequent intervals. As food issues can be major sources of contention in prison, this is an important area. They can also inquire into a prisoner's mental or physical health and check whether imprisonment is affecting his/her condition. Another important role is that of acting as an independent observer or witness in the event of a serious incident or disturbance in the prison. Members take up a wide range of prisoner and staff concerns during their visits and make their views known through a monthly meeting with the governor, an annual report to the Secretary of State, and, where appropriate, through the media.

Members perform an important role as a 'watchdog' or 'observer' body. As public representatives they have a significant part to play in overseeing the daily running of prisons, without being paid employees, or having any managerial involvement. The freedom which they have to visit any part of the prison gives them opportunity to listen to prisoners and staff in a unique way. At a time when prisons seem to be becoming more punitive, in response to the political and public mood, the task laid before Boards is even more important. Issues of justice, fair treatment and abuses need to be firmly held in focus. Many members act as a 'sounding-board' for staff, and they are able to challenge decisions and practices often taken for granted within the prison. Such challenges can only be a healthy contribution to reflection on role and belief.

Lord, we hold before you
the work of members of
Independent Monitoring Boards.
As they are entrusted
with responsibility for
inspecting prisons,
may they do so with
an eye for justice,
a heart for those

who have hurt,
and may themselves be hurt;
with an integrity
which is for the
common good.

Prison visitors

Week on week in most prisons in England and Wales, men and women form relationships with prisoners, officially, and with the encouragement of the Ministry of Justice. At present there are about 1500 such visitors, over half of whom are members of the National Association of Official Prison Visitors.

The relationships formed are about friendship between people of equal status – there can be no 'them and us'. Visitors see people, not 'problems' or 'prisoners'. They have a role in providing for the personal growth and development of people in prison. Prison Visitors are all volunteers and they help provide a continuing link with the wider community, a listening ear, an opportunity for conversation which may rise above the immediacy of the prison context, and in which the value of each person is affirmed.

The history of prison visiting goes back as far as the beginnings of prison, but it is only in the last couple of centuries, with the development of prisons as we know them, that the work of prison visitors has taken its present course. People such as John Wesley, the father of Methodism, and Elizabeth Fry, Quaker and Prison Reformer, have been amongst the notable men and women involved.

Whilst in many prisons the Chaplain acts as the Prison Visitor Liaison Officer, volunteers are selected on their ability to be good listeners and to carry on conversation, and not because of any religious interest they might have. People of all faith traditions, and none, are encouraged to apply.

Many prisoners have been grateful for the friendship offered, and received, by Prison Visitors, and the value of such service is enormous for short-term as well as long-term prisoners.

One Prison Visitor writes that this role

can be exciting, exhilarating, and can leave one with a sense of fulfilment. It can also be boring, frustrating and sometimes leaves me with a sense of failure. For a long time prior to starting as a Visitor, I was interested in penal matters, but I have never been an idealist. Sometimes I think I am guilty of idealism, and I keep a constant check on it, reminding myself that I am a 'visitor', and like all visitors, am 'invited' in by the prisoner, to his home – the prison. If I had any ideas about being a 'reformer', or I wanted to change the prison system, then I very definitely ought not to be a Prison Visitor.

Over the last few years I have visited men whose crimes have been as different as their personalities and each time the challenge is the same – forming a friendship between two people who, under normal circumstances, would never have been brought together. Sometimes one is lucky – immediately we 'click' and the conversation flows. At other times, though, it is uphill work and I feel we will never find enough in common to get the relationship off the ground. At other times, there is a breakthrough in what had been, up until then, an exchange of pleasant formalities.

What I think I offer as a Prison Visitor is my weakness and my frailty, my vulnerability. A relationship based on vulnerability has little time for conventions. It is more real, more challenging, and sometimes more enjoyable. Maybe 'enjoyment' is a key word in prison visiting and there is a very real pleasure in hearing a man bowed down with the weight of his crimes and his life in prison, laugh out loud with delight. There needs to be an acceptance of things as they are, here and now. We are not reformers, but transformers, though even that may be over-idealistic. We are there to offer the hand of friendship, sympathise (but never to say the patronising, 'I know just how you feel', as we don't, and we never will), and, above all, to believe in someone who no longer believes in himself.

... clothe yourselves with compassion, kindness, humility, meekness and patience.

Colossians 3:12b

God of compassion,
you call us to
the difficult and joyful
task of friendship.

We give you thanks
for the gift of being
able to listen to other people,
and to you.

We pray for the work
of all Prison Visitors
as they seek to befriend,
to share, and to express
their care for prisoners.

Enable them,
in word and action
to express their belief
in the value of each person;
to affirm the dignity
and individuality
of those they serve,
and to be gracious
in generous listening.

Volunteers

The Gospel imperative, so clearly set out by Jesus in Matthew 25:31f, has encouraged Christians through the ages to be involved in ministry with the marginalised in society. The Churches Criminal Justice Forum (www.ccjf.org.uk) identifies three types of participation in the work of the criminal justice system:

Firstly, many Christians are professionally employed in different parts of the system, and express their faith through the values and skills they bring to bear in their daily work. They deserve the prayers and support of their fellow Christians in a demanding vocation.

Secondly, many Christians work in a voluntary capacity in secular organisations, from Prison Visitors to Youth Offending Teams. Like the first group, they bear witness through their actions and relationships.

Thirdly, Prison Service Chaplaincy has identified that almost 7000 volunteers and 460 faith-based organisations are active in prisons, and the corresponding numbers in the community are considerable. Volunteers are involved in a wide range of activities.

I think that Pierre Allard, the former Director of Chaplaincy in the Correctional Services of Canada, has put the point extremely well in relation to volunteers:

> The myth that Chaplains can fulfil their ministry of reconciliation without the help of the larger faith community must be forever dispelled. However talented, however powerfully empowered by the Spirit, however strongly mandated by their churches, Chaplains must

realize the communal dimension of the new covenant, and their own limitations in representing the outside community ... Those who have experienced forgiveness from God must also experience forgiveness, acceptance, reconciliation from their brothers and sisters outside the walls. In the same vein, volunteers are not a nice addition or a passing fad. They are an integral part of the Chaplains' ministry.

For me, volunteers must be an integral part of the whole community of prison. Prisoners come from the wider community, and virtually all will return to that community.

God, who in Christ
called others to ministry,
we give you thanks
for the life, witness,
and ministry
of all who volunteer.
We give thanks that they
commit themselves
to love, which transforms,
to forgiveness, which heals,
to respect, which encourages,
to hope, which is grounded in you.

Information

For more information about the churches' involvement with the Criminal Justice System, and for information about different opportunities to become a volunteer, visit: www.whatcanido.org.uk

Welcome the stranger

As part of the preparation of people for release from prison, chaplains are sometimes able to commend a prisoner to a particular church and congregation. It is a difficult area for some churches, particularly, those regarded as being in the mainstream. Congregations are not always sure how to cope with the presence of a former prisoner.

It was the Monday morning reception interviews in the Young Offender Institution. Bruce was a tall, well-built and impressive 18-year-old, who had a quiet confidence about him. He had been in prison before and he could almost give the answers before I asked the questions.

We were progressing along well until I asked him if he had any connections with the Church outside. 'Funny you should say that,' he replied. 'Last time I was in prison, I was working in the gardens when an officer came and told me to change into my best kit because the Vicar had come to see me. I had never met my Vicar before but when we sat talking to each other we got on well.

'When I was discharged I thought, since the Vicar came to see me, I ought to go and see him. I had never been to church before so I put on my best jeans and T-shirt. I found it hard to go into church on my own but I managed to make my way to the back pew and waited for someone to come to me. Some ladies were talking and they looked at me but carried on speaking to each other.

'Eventually, the service began. I would have liked to have joined in but no one gave me any books. I thought they would be pleased to see me but at the end of the service everyone went home and no one said a word to me.'

Bruce concluded by saying, 'There's more love in my criminal friends than in your Christian Church.'

Subsequently, he re-offended and was given a long sentence. Maybe it would have been a different story had he found more love in the Christian Church than in his criminal friends.

... I was a stranger and you welcomed me.

Matthew 25:35b

Lord, in your Son
you show us how you greet
the stranger and the outcast
with compassion.
As we seek to exercise
a ministry of welcome
in your name, we ask
for a spirit of acceptance
and tolerance which reflects
your love and grace
for all your people.

Community Chaplaincy

Community Chaplaincy has its origin in Canada. It was adapted for use in England and Wales in 2001. It is an attempt to continue the work that Prison Chaplains have done with individuals in custody, as they prepare for release into the community, and after release. It works in partnership with other resettlement agencies, maximising the current policy and theories concerning reducing re-offending and protecting the public, whilst bringing the faith communities' resources as 'added value' to the agenda. In this section the first Community Chaplain in England and Wales writes about its theory and practice.

Despite the rhetoric, opening the Pandora's box of prisoner reintegration remains a fraught, complicated and near-impossible ideal to realise. Any challenge that starts with disenfranchised individuals who exhibit vulnerability in employment, accommodation, relationships, and a whole host of other areas, combined with returning them to unsure, compromised localities and circumstances, might be said to be doomed to failure before it starts. No single agency or system can realistically address the diverse set of issues facing many offenders and Community Chaplaincy does not seek to do so in isolation. It seeks to do so in 'faith' and through partnership working, as it accompanies individuals in the bridging process from custody to community. It attempts to marry the 'practice of rehabilitation' to the 'language of rehabilitation'.

Community Chaplaincy accepts a responsibility towards rehabilitation to ensure that neither the individual nor the community is disadvantaged; it focuses on the individual and the needs they have, to enable them to lead crime-free lives. The advantages of an offender becoming an active participant in their own rehabilitation become a major strength as the resettlement issues are seen from the offender's perception rather through another's eyes or influence. This helps the offender think of themselves as an active, valuable individual contributing to their own resettlement.

Sam's story is typical of many:

> My life now is so different to the one I once lived, the one that I still have so many regrets and hurts about, but these areas continue to be addressed and worked on in order to fulfil my desire of living a more fulfilling, rewarding and peaceful life!
>
> I have known my Community Chaplain, Alan, for a number of years, more recently on my last sentence. At the beginning of my sentence I was on remand for some time before I received the news that I was going to serve four years in prison for my crime. This came as a big shock to me and left me feeling very down. I knew that if I accepted Community Chaplaincy support I would not be left to deal with it on my own and I knew I had someone to discuss my lifestyle with who was genuinely concerned about my life and well-being. I was treated as a real person and treated with respect. This is not to say that other agencies didn't care, but this man met me where I actually was, not where he thought I was at that difficult time in my life! It was nice to know I could be myself with him and not wonder if judgement would fall on me, given my background.
>
> We focused on the future with release and beyond in mind. Where would I go? What would I do? Would someone employ me? What will life deal me now? I was then transferred to another prison to complete my sentence. Alan kept in contact and I was released to a local Bail Hostel where I stayed for three months. I was terrified with the thought of being sent back to live in my home town as I felt that there was nothing but trouble waiting there for me and I wasn't ready to go back. I fought to have my probation licence changed to live locally, with

the sure hope of a new start and employment in sight, as I had been seeking employment in the construction field, with certificates to operate heavy machinery; I could also set up accommodation to call my home. The struggle was worth it and my licence conditions were changed. I had no local connection so had to find privately rented accommodation fast – if I didn't, then returning to my home town was the only option. Alan went with me to all the housing agencies and I signed up with them all in the hope of finding a place of my own. Nothing came up and I went into panic mode as my time at the Bail Hostel was running out.

My time at the Bail Hostel had ended and given that I hadn't yet found suitable accommodation, I was placed in a B&B out of town. My stay was limited there so I urgently needed to find somewhere else. I couldn't travel regularly so Alan made enquiries with landlords on my behalf. Then the news came: 'Would you like a place of your own?' This was great news! Now I had a chance to prove myself. The Community Chaplaincy Project pulled some strings and managed to secure a bond for the flat for me. The flat needed refurbishing and decorating – where would I start? I was constantly encouraged to 'keep the bigger picture in mind.' Alan helped me and empowered me to approach this whole thing with a positive attitude, but it was hard at times. I scraped, filled, sanded, painted and painted again, papered and tiled. Carpets went down, pictures on the wall, food in the fridge. Resources were limited regarding furnishing the flat, but again Alan used all his contacts and got things together for me. All this was mine, my own home at last! This was my desire!

Now I had a stable home and a permanent address, I could really knuckle down and try to find employment. I applied for many jobs and was then offered one. My hard work had all been worth it and now I could earn an honest living.

How life has changed for me! I am grateful for the opportunities given to me since release. I am grateful for the support I have received from Alan, as without him my situation would have been very difficult to cope with. Community Chaplaincy treated me as a real person, gave me space to talk about my feelings, thoughts, fears and plans for the future, and through this I was able to deal with the past and focus on the future, with the bigger picture in view. I am now happier and have a more positive approach to life. I visit my family back home regularly and they in turn visit me. They are proud of me now and of my achievements since I was released and it feels so good to know that, and to be part of a family again.

Sometimes life is still difficult but it could be a lot worse. I may not be exactly where I want to be in life but I am a long way from where I was. I couldn't have done it alone!

Community Chaplaincy majors in relationships and the significance of the chaplain–offender relationship is the primary factor to engagement, change and success. The chaplain's belief in the offender is paramount – the belief that change is possible and that he or she, as chaplain, is committed to helping bring about that change both in the good and bad times. Many of the interventions provided by Community Chaplaincy are mirror images of what non-faith bodies could and do provide, yet in a unique way the respect and integrity of Community Chaplaincy, without being quantifiable, appears to unlock horizons for many people who have given up hope. All faith communities have huge potential to create pro-social support networks of people who have a pro-social way of thinking and behaving. As pro-social people of faith, Community Chaplaincy offers holistic support to all prisoners, irrespective of their personal faith.

At a time when the prison population has grown to a level where new establishments are being brought into operation, where a new breed of prisons known as large prison complexes (capacity for 2500 prisoners) is being talked about, Community Chaplaincy battles to be heard amongst the policy-makers, sentencers, scaremongers and 'crime concerned' media and population. Community Chaplaincy is not founded on the common assumption that individuals are passive and open to manipulation and control; rather, all of the progress made since 2001 has been as a result of active players demonstrating their desire to engage and push the boundaries further. Community Chaplaincy is serious about the transition process that individuals journey down, whereby they, their families and communities need to reshape their understanding if everyone is to successfully 'bridge custody to community'.

> *Lord of hope and restoration,*
> *our prisons are filled with people who have lost their way,*
> *who are hurt, and have hurt.*
> *Help those who are committed to supporting them to 'start*
> *   again'.*
>
> *In working together, give strength and clarity of thought*
> *in complicated and difficult times.*
>
> *Be with those who walk through the prison gate*
> *to freedom and responsibility.*
> *Help them to see a positive future to focus on and strive for;*
> *give them a hope that they may not have experienced before.*
>
> *Lord, be at the centre of Community Chaplaincy;*
> *may its ministry grow*
> *as you shine your 'light' in 'dark' places and 'dark' lives.*
> *In all things we trust in you and your unfailing love for all.*

Information
Chaplaincy HQ/NOMS has funded a Community Chaplaincy Development Officer post to help develop the concept and coherence of Community Chaplaincy at a national level.

Release

Erwin James attended our national chaplaincy conference to speak about the experience of imprisonment, from a prisoner's viewpoint. To use the rather clumsy jargon, he was a 'service-user', having served 20 years of a life sentence. He spoke realistically and movingly about many aspects of prison life. We had first met in the early years of his sentence, introduced by a colleague, a psychologist, who worked hard to convince him of his value as a person. Always impressive, he had made the very best of his time in prison, providing insights on prison life in his regular column, 'A Life Inside', published fortnightly and then weekly in The Guardian *newspaper as he served his time and prepared for release.*

In this short piece, originally written for The Guardian, *he conveys something of his resettlement experience, infused with a sense of hope that helped sustain him over the years.*

By the time I was released from prison, I was no stranger to the modern world. I knew my way around mobile phones and cash machines, internet cafes and lattes to go as well as anyone. Thanks to my time in the resettlement prison, I was a seasoned commuter and city worker, who blended unnoticed into the pavement throng long before I was actually freed. But for all the time I spent on my own on the outside, I never lost the feeling of being a prisoner.

That did not happen until I walked out of the gate for the last time. Only then did it feel as if the invisible cloak I had been wearing had been lifted from my shoulders. It was a great feeling, although if I am honest I had not expected to experience any great sense of change once the exhilaration brought on by my release had passed. That is the idea behind a resettlement programme – the smooth transition from captivity to freedom: a graded reintroduction to the outside world. I am glad I had it. It must be a real struggle without it.

I remember once seeing a young man being released from a category C, medium-security prison in Cambridgeshire when I worked there as the reception orderly. He had only been in a couple of years, yet he told me he was scared to death of going back out. I made him a mug of sweet tea to try to calm his nerves as we sat together in the glass-panelled holding room during his final half hour. 'The crazy thing is,' he said, 'I'm just as terrified of being in here.' I didn't fancy his chances.

When my time came I was lucky that I had a home to go to and a job with colleagues who already accepted me for who I was. There was a ready-made routine waiting for me, but after work, instead of going back to the prison, I now go home. No more searches (and occasionally getting found out trying to smuggle in fresh milk for my morning cornflakes) or dependence on others to open locked doors and gates before and after my day at the office.

While it was true that the dual role of citizen by day and convict by night and weekend had been increasingly tiring over the final months, I never stopped reminding myself how lucky I was. Relatively few people get the opportunities that I had at the end of such a long prison sentence. Even fewer are as well prepared as I was to take advantage of them. Best of all was my good health. Even though I had done my best to look after myself in there, the fact that I was so healthy after such a long time in prison was purely down to good fortune.

I have never minded having those 20 years taken from me. I was never convinced of their value as punishment at the time and looking at them now from the other end I am convinced even less. But they had to be done and I am glad I was able to make the most of them. If I had not had them taken away, they would most likely have been wasted anyway. The strangest thing is that most of the time now it does not feel as if I was ever in prison. I am not sure if that is because mentally I managed to keep myself healthily detached from the regime when I was in there, or because I have had so much to do since I have been out.

Unless I am writing about it, or it comes up in conversation, thoughts about my life inside have not been dominating my mind. There is only one un-summoned memory that lingers. It is of an event that occurred around 15 or 16 years ago. My cell then was a reinforced concrete box and I spent the biggest part of my days locked behind its steel door. I spent a lot of time reading and meditating on what I had read, until the fear and anxiety I had felt from being held in those conditions gradually subsided. My reading and thinking took me to places that I never knew existed before prison. I could not say exactly when it happened – and I am not sure that I realized it until some-time afterwards – but there was definitely a period in that cell when for the first time in my life I experienced peace.

I had not expected to miss any aspects of my imprisonment when I had been released. But more than once during these past few weeks of being out and about full-time in the modern world, I have missed that.

God of presence,
in the midst of
our fear and anxiety
enable us to create a space
into which you might enter
and find us,
a space where we may
find peace in you.

A Prison Litany

Litany, as a form of intercessory prayer, has been part of Christian worship and devotion since at least the second half of the fourth century. It is a flexible and valuable way of encouraging effective congregational participation in the liturgy as well as comprehensively embracing areas for prayer. It is not, however, used as much as it might be.

Two former prison chaplains have produced a Litany which reflects the intercessory needs of the prison context. It can be used as a whole, or in appropriate parts.

For the ministry that God has called us to among prisoners and members of staff, let us pray to the Lord.

God the Father,
have mercy on us.
God the Son,
have mercy on us.
God the Holy Spirit,
have mercy on us.
Holy, blessed and glorious Trinity whose unity draws us together,
have mercy on us.
From all evil and mischief; from pride, vanity and hypocrisy; from envy, hatred and malice, and from all evil intent,
good Lord deliver us.
From laziness, worldliness and love of money; from hardness of heart and contempt for your word and laws,
good Lord deliver us.
From the sins of body and mind; from all the deceits of the world, the flesh and the devil, and from anger and violence in word and deed,
good Lord deliver us.

The needs of those inside

For those in prison for the first time and for the families and friends from whom they are separated. Lord, in your mercy,
hear our prayer.

For those made hard and cynical by life in prison; for those who feel no sorrow for what they have done, and for those who are thinking of further crime. Lord, in your mercy,
hear our prayer.

For those who break the good order and discipline of prison life; for those in the Segregation Unit; and for those seeking protection. Lord, in your mercy,
hear our prayer.

For those who create anxiety and fear; for the weak who are abused by the strong; for those who desperately long to be accepted; for the unloved and the unwanted who receive neither letter nor visit. Lord, in your mercy,
hear our prayer.

For those whose faith in Christ is mocked; for those who are taunted for going to Chapel, for reading the Bible and praying; for those who by their false and evil beliefs lead the simple away from the truth in Christ. Lord, in your mercy,
hear our prayer.

For those who stand firm in the faith and witness to Christ in word and in deed. Lord, in your mercy,
hear our prayer.

The needs of those outside

For those who are victims of crime, and who suffer and are hurt. Lord hear us.
Lord, graciously hear us.

For those who depend on alcohol to give them courage or to drown their misery, and for those whose lives and families have been destroyed through alcohol abuse. Lord, hear us.
Lord, graciously hear us.

For those who are addicted to drugs, and for those who sell them. Lord, hear us.

Lord, graciously hear us.

For those contemplating crime today; for those arrested and taken to the cells for the first time in their lives. Lord, hear us.

Lord, graciously hear us.

For those who advise the innocent to plead guilty; for those who have abandoned hope of a fair trial, and for those who are the victims of rough justice. Lord, hear us.

Lord, graciously hear us.

For the partners and families of prisoners as they suffer the 'second sentence', the loneliness of separation and the difficulties of visiting. Lord, hear us.

Lord, graciously hear us.

For those who are worried about the lack of money and the debts they have incurred. For those who deprive themselves for the benefit of their children and their partner in prison. Lord, hear us.

Lord, graciously hear us.

Christian ministry

For those who through word and deed bring true humanity to relationships and show compassion to the needs of others; let us bless the Lord.

Thanks be to God.

For those whose thoughts turn into prayer and whose prayer turns into action; let us bless the Lord.

Thanks be to God.

For all who show forth the gifts of the Spirit in love, joy, peace; for those who are patient, good, gentle, self-controlled and faithful; let us bless the Lord.

Thanks be to God.

For those whose love bears all things, hopes all things, endures all things, whose love never ends; let us bless the Lord.

Thanks be to God.

Lord, make us instruments of your peace.
Where there is hatred, let us give your love.
Where there is injury, pardon.

Where there is doubt, faith.
Where there is despair, hope.
Where there is sadness, joy.
Where there is darkness, light.

For in giving we receive.
in pardoning we are pardoned,
and in dying we are born into eternal life.

Glossary

This Glossary is intended to help readers understand some of the terms, expressions and prison slang used within this book. Some entries are not used within the text, but may be of interest to readers. It does not pretend to be exhaustive.

ABH: Actual Bodily Harm.

Absconded: Failure to return from Release on Temporary Licence, or has gone missing from an open prison, or outside working party.

ACCT: Assessment, Care in Custody, Teamwork.

Adjudication: An internal disciplinary hearing by the Governor following alleged breach of prison rules.

Adult Offender: Any person sentenced to imprisonment and over the age of 21 years.

Allocation: The decision about the prison appropriate to a particular prisoner.

'A' Man: An inmate in Category A classification (see 'Classification').

APVS: Assisted Prison Visits Scheme, under which immediate relatives may have the cost of their visit paid, subject to their being on a sufficiently low income.

Association: Recreation time for prisoners, normally at weekends and evenings.

ACR: Automatic Conditional Release, for prisoners serving 12 months to under 4 years. They are released automatically at the half-way point and are supervised until the three-quarters point of sentence (or to the very end in the case of some sex-offenders), and will be 'at risk' until the very end of the sentence, should they commit a further imprisonable offence before the end of the original sentence. The court dealing with the new offence may add all or part of the outstanding sentence to any new sentence it imposes. (See 'AUR' and 'DCR'.)

AUR: Automatic Unconditional Release. Prisoners serving less than 12 months are released automatically half-way through the sentence. No supervision applies, but they are 'at risk' (see above) for the second half of the sentence.

Banged up, or bang-up: Prison slang for being locked in cell.

Bird: Prison slang for the length of a sentence.

Block: Prison slang for the Segregation Unit (see 'Segregation Unit').

C&R: Control and Restraint. An approved technique used for control purposes on individual prisoners.

Canteen: The prison shop, where prisoners can purchase certain items and goods.

CARATS: Counselling, Assessment, Referral, Advice and Through-care services.

CC: Confined to Cell.

Cell card: The card at the entrance to a cell, indicating the name of the occupant/s.

Censor: The Officer designated to examine incoming and outgoing mail to ensure that it does not contain 'contraband' or break any other prison rule.

Centre: According to the size and complexity of a prison, and normally situated at ground level and in a central position, used as a regulating office for movement and control within the establishment.

CIT: Construction industry training, provided for prisoners.

Civil prisoner: A person in prison for contempt of court, for debt or for failure to comply with a court order (except an order to pay a fine on conviction), and for no other reason.

Classification, security:

Category 'A': those whose escape would be highly dangerous to the public, the police or the security of the State, and for whom the aim must be to make escape impossible.

Category 'B': those for whom the highest conditions of security are not necessary, but for whom escape must be made very difficult.

Category 'C': those who cannot be trusted in open conditions, but who are without the ability or resources to make a determined bid to escape.

Category 'D': those who can be trusted in open conditions.

CNA: Certified Normal Accommodation – the number of prisoners that any establishment will hold without exceeding the number of places. In effect, it is the number of places in a prison, before overcrowding takes place.

Committal: The process by which a court orders the detention of a person, whether convicted or not, in legal custody.

Control: The maintenance of order within a prison. It should not be confused with security. (See 'Security'.)

Control Room: Sometimes known as the Communications Room, or Comms Room, it is a centre for information and the monitoring of prisoner movement. In times of emergency it may be used as the central point of control.

CRO: The Criminal Record Office.

Crown Court: The higher court, used for trying more serious criminal cases, hearing appeals from the Magistrates' Courts, and also for passing sentence on those cases referred by the Magistrates' Courts. The best known Crown Court is the Central Criminal Court – popularly known as the 'Old Bailey', and located in London.

CSC: Close Supervision Centre – small units for highly disruptive prisoners.

DCR: Discretionary Conditional Release relates to prisoners serving four years or more. They become eligible for parole at the half-way point. They may be released on parole at any point between half-way and two-thirds. Release at two-thirds is automatic, but is on a licence that runs to the three-quarters point (or to the end for some sex-offenders). They will be 'at risk' (see 'ACR') until the end of their sentence.

Discharge Grant: A sum of money given to a prisoner at the time of release in order to help with the expenses of the first few days of release. A travel warrant to the person's place of abode is also issued. A slightly higher grant is given to those without a 'home' to go to.

Discipline Office: The section of management services which deals with all matters relating to prisoners' documentation and records.

DOM: Director of Offender Management, of whom there are ten, covering nine regions and Wales. Each DOM is accountable for all prison and probation delivery, working with prisons (public and private sector) and through probation boards or Trusts.

DSPD: Dangerous and Severe Personality Disorder.

DSU: Drug Strategy Unit.

ECHR: European Court for Human Rights.

ECR: The Emergency Control Room, to be found in all high security prisons; it contains communication and monitoring equipment and is staffed 24 hours a day.

'E' List: A prisoner who has shown, by actual escapes, or determined escape attempts, that he/she constitutes an escape risk, is placed on the 'E' List. Procedures are then put in place to monitor that prisoner.

Escape: from inside a closed prison, or from a prison escort or bed-watch.

Escort: The officers who accompany a prisoner when he leaves the prison to attend a funeral, visit a sick relative, etc. Escort officers are responsible for the prisoner's safe custody.

Gander: A capping device for the perimeter wall of a prison as part of its security.

GBH: Grievous Bodily Harm.

Ghosting: Prison slang for the transferring of a prisoner from one prison to another at very short notice.

GOD or GOAD: refers to a prisoner placed in confinement, by the governor, under the provision of Rule 45 (or Rule 49 for young Offenders), in the interests of 'good order and discipline'.

Her Majesty's Pleasure: A young person under the age of 18 is detained at 'Her Majesty's Pleasure'. The Secretary of State for Justice currently decides the period of time.

High Security Prisons: Closed and highly secure prisons holding convicted prisoners, usually including Category 'A' of standard, high or exceptional risk status.

IEP: Incentives and Earned Privileges: a scheme for prisoners aimed to encourage responsible behaviour and participation in constructive activity.

Independent Monitoring Board: The independent 'watchdog' body appointed by the Secretary of State.

Inspectorate of Prisons: An independent body, headed by Her Majesty's Inspector of Prisons, which inspects prisons, aspects of prison life and, at the Secretary of State for Justice's request, particular incidents. Reports are published.

JR: Judgement Respited, often referred to as Judge's Remand, where a person is sentenced by the court to custody (or released on bail) pending the next stage of his trial, or the passing of sentence.

Knock-back: Prison slang for the unfavourable outcome of an adjudication, application for bail, or any request within the system.

KPI: Key Performance Indicator.

KPT: Key Performance Target.

Landing: One of the 'floors' in a prison, often referred to simply by number, 'the ones', 'the twos', 'the threes', 'the fours'.

Landing Officer: One of the officers responsible for prisoners on a particular landing.

Licence: The document which authorises the release of a prisoner before the end of his/her sentence, and sets out the conditions of release. Life-sentence prisoners have a 'life licence'.

Local Prison: A closed prison which receives prisoners from the courts on remand and under sentence. Servicing the courts, they are also responsible for the initial classification of prisoners. Some will also hold short-term convicted prisoners and may have a wing for young offenders, or for women.

Location: A prisoner's 'address' within the prison – e.g. C4.06 means the sixth cell on the fourth floor of 'C' Wing.

MAPPA: Multi-Agency Public Protection Arrangements.

Magistrate's Court: The lower court where the majority of cases are dealt with, and which forwards to the higher court (see 'Crown Court') on indictment more serious cases, as well as those which are thought to deserve a more severe penalty than the lower court can impose.

Mechanical restraints: Handcuffs, leather body-belts and leather ankle-straps, used with the written permission of the governor, and loose canvas dress, used with the written authority of the medical officer, for the control of violent prisoners, when absolutely necessary.

MUFTI: Minimum Use of Force Tactical Intervention. A system introduced in 1978 by which officers, wearing protective clothing, aim to control a riot, or near-riot, situation with the minimum amount of force required. (See 'C&R'.)

NOMS: The National Offender Management Service. The organisation that joins up prisons and probation to enable Offender Management to be delivered more easily, and to strengthen and streamline commissioning to improve service efficiency and effectiveness.

Nonce: Prison slang for a sex-offender. Originally derived from 'Not on normal communal exercise'.

OASys: Offender Assessment System.

OCA Unit: The Observation, Classification and Allocation Unit which exists in all local prisons to assess sentenced inmates.

On Report: A prisoner awaiting adjudication because he has been charged with an offence against internal discipline.

OR: A prisoner segregated under the provision of Rule 45, at his 'own request', usually because he feels threatened by others because of the nature of his offence, or his behaviour inside (e.g. grassing, failing to pay debts to a 'baron').

Orderly: A trusted prisoner who works in areas such as the Chapel. (See 'Red-Band'.)

Parole: Refers to release on licence. See 'AUR', 'ACR' and 'DCR'.

PRES: Pre-Release Employment Scheme, whereby selected long-term and life-sentence prisoners may live in separate, hostel accommodation, outside the prison, from where they go out to work for outside employers.

POELT: Prison Officer Entry Level Training.

Production: The 'delivery' of a prisoner to court for trial or sentence.

Protective clothing: Unisex tunic and shorts made of untearable material.

Property: A prisoner's possessions, usually kept in the reception area.

PSO: Prison Service Order – mandatory instructions on procedures and policy in a particular subject area.

REAT: Race Equality Action Team. See 'REO'.

Reception: The area where all new prisoners are 'received' into the prison; where they shower, are medically examined, given their number and provided with their prison clothing etc. It is also a way of referring both to the process the newcomer undergoes ('he is on reception') and the newcomer himself ('there were five receptions last night').

Reception Board: On the morning after reception, a board, which usually includes a governor grade or Principal Officer, meet new receptions, verifying basic information about them and making initial decisions with regard to security category, and possibly, location. They also give information to the prisoner about practical matters of routine.

Reception Letter: A free letter issued on the day after reception so that a prisoner may write to a relative, friend, etc.

Recidivist: A person who constantly re-offends and returns to prison.

Red-Band: A prisoner trusted to work in areas such as the library, chapel etc.

Region: There are nine regions, and Wales. Each region is the responsibility of the Director of Offender Management (DOM) who ensures the delivery of NOMS' Standards and specifications for the prison and probation services.

Regional Manager: The Regional Manager Custodial Services is accountable to the Director of Offender Management for the delivery of custodial services (public and private sector).

Remand Centre: An establishment, or a particular wing in a local prison, which accommodates those people, especially youngsters under 21 years of age, who are awaiting trial or, having been tried, are awaiting sentence or allocation.

REO: Race Equality Officer. A member of staff (e.g. a Senior Manager, Principal or Senior Officer) who is deputed by the governor and trained by the Prison Service to act as the focal point for all race equality matters.

Respect: A Prison Service support network for black and minority ethnic staff.

Rule 45s: Prisoners segregated either because they are judged to be a serious threat to good order and discipline, or for the sake of their own protection, in accordance with Prison Rule 45 (a) and (b), respectively.

Screws: Prison slang for Prison Officers.

Search, rub-down: A light body search over the clothing.

Search, strip: A more thorough and intimate search of the person and clothing.

Security: Measures designed to prevent escapes from security. Also, those responsible for security.

Security Officer: A senior member of staff holding responsibility for all aspects of security within a prison.

Segregation (or Seg) Unit: A wing, or group of cells, isolated from the main prison accommodation, for the use of prisoners under punishment.

Special Accommodation: Usually in the prison Health Centre or Segregation Unit, this room has only built-in furniture, with flush internal surfaces to eliminate sharp edges etc., or features which could be used as suspension points. In prison slang, 'the strip'.

SSU: Special Secure Unit – a high-security unit within an already very secure prison.

Strip-cell: See 'Special Accommodation'.

Tally: A token, usually metal, given in exchange for keys and returned when keys are surrendered.

Throughcare: The care provided for an offender from the time of arrest until release, and afterwards.

TOIL: Time off in lieu.

TWOC: Taking (a vehicle) without the owner's consent.

VFM: Value for money.

VIR: Viral infectivity restrictions: an indication of the presence of Hepatitis B, C, HIV positive etc.

Visit: The opportunity for a prisoner to be visited by a relative, friend, solicitor etc.

Visit, Closed: Where there is a clear partition of glass, reinforced plastic or wire-mesh between the prisoner and his visitor(s).

Visit, Open: Where the prisoner is seated at a table, usually continuous, with relatives etc. on the other side. Limited physical contact is possible.

VO: A Visiting Order, or pass issued to a prisoner and sent to his relatives or friends allowing the admission of three visitors plus his children.

Vulnerable Prisoners: Prisoners on Rule 45 or, in the case of a Young Offender, Rule 49.

VPU: The Vulnerable Prisoner Unit. In some prisons this may be a special group of cells, or a separate unit, away from the main accommodation.

Weighed off: Prison slang meaning 'adjudicated by the Governor'.

Wing: One of the main accommodation areas in a prison.

Young Offender: The term used to cover all young prisoners under 21 years of age. Those who are 14 are known as children, those between 15 and 17 as young persons, and those between 17 and 21 as young adults.

Young Offender Institution: The Criminal Justice Act (1988) created a single custodial sentence for young offenders to be known as 'detention in a young offender institution'.

YJB: Youth Justice Board.

Notes

1. Oscar Wilde, originally published under the pseudonym C3.3 (C Wing, 3rd level, 3rd cell).
2. Erving Goffman, *Asylums* (Penguin, 1961).
3. Karl Rahner, *Mission and Grace*, Vol. iii (Sheed & Ward Stagbooks, 1966).
4. Kenneth Leech, *True Prayer* (Sheldon Press, 1980), p. 6.
5. Rowan Williams, Prison Reform Trust lecture, www.arch bishopofcanterbury.org
6. 'Snuff' films usually show the sexual abuse, torture and murder of young people.
7. Michael Hollings and Eta Gullick, *It's Me, O Lord* (Mayhew & McCrimmon, 1972).
8. Richard Ellman, *Oscar Wilde* (Hamish Hamilton, 1987), p. 454.
9. Quoted by Little Brother Peter in *Jesus Caritas*, no. 58, p. 33.
10. Canon Eric James, *Judge Not* (Christian Action, 1989).
11. William Trevor, *Felicia's Journey* (Penguin, 1995), p. 212.
12. Brian Wren, extract from 'I come with joy' from *Piece Together Praise*, © 1971, 1995 Hope Publishing Company for the USA, Canada, Australia and New Zealand, and Stainer & Bell Ltd, London, for all other territories.
13. Dietrich Bonhoeffer, *Life Together* (SCM Press, 1975).
14. Frank Lake, *Clinical Theology*, abr. Martin Yeomans (DLT, 1986).
15. Max Warren, former General Secretary, CMS.
16. For more information visit: www.aviddetention.org.uk
17. This is a reference to psychologists and therapists.
18. From *A New Zealand Prayer Book*, adapted and to be found in *Human Rites*, compiled by Hannah Ward and Jennifer Wild (Mowbray, 1995).
19. Pierre Raphael, 'The Chaplain's Prayer for Breath', in *Inside Riker's Island* (Maryknoll, NY, Orbis Books, 1990), p. 28.
20. Dietrich Bonhoeffer, *Letters and Papers from Prison*, ed. Eberhard Bethge (SCM Press, 1971), p. 360.
21. L. Gregory Jones, *Embodying Forgiveness* (Grand Rapids, MI, Wm. B. Eerdmans, 1995), p. xii.
22. Bo Lozoff, *We're All Doing Time* (Human Kindness Foundation, 1985).

Who will separate us from the love of Christ? Will hardship, or distress, or persecution, or famine, or nakedness, or peril, or sword? As it is written,

> *For your sake we are being killed all day long;*
> *we are accounted as sheep to be slaughtered.*

No, in all these things we are more than conquerors through him who loved us. For I am convinced that neither death nor life, nor angels, nor things present, nor things to come, nor powers, nor height, nor depth, nor anything else in all creation, will be able to separate us from the love of God in Christ Jesus our Lord.

Romans 8:35–39

Index

special needs 92
Special Rapporteur on Torture 57
spiritual roots 46–53
spreadsheets 253
spy-holes 75
Sri Lanka 148
Stafford Prison 222
Stanmore Synagogue 52
Statement of Purpose 27, 90
Statutory Duties 38
step-parents 79, 180–1, 227
stigmatisation 101, 201
stock control 253
Storr, Anthony 180
stress 155, 157, 173, 235, 245–6
strip cell 103, 223–5
strip-searching 64
subjugation 183
substance misuse 82, 139
suicide 49, 111, 130, 139, 144–5,
147–52, 172–3, 186, 201, 224,
240, 254
supervision 56, 78, 91, 158
Support After Murder and Manslaughter (SAMM) 202–6
Supporting Offenders through
Restoration Inside Prison
(SORI) 230–1
surgeries 242
Sutcliffe, Peter 178, 180
sweat-boxes 63, 101

tabloids 88
taking leave 219
Tanakh 133
tariff 91–2, 242
tax-collectors 31
Taylor, Fred 63–4
teachers 223, 240, 249–54
telephones 239
television 19, 37, 152
Temple, William 102

Teresa, Mother 116
Terrorism Act 150
Thames Valley 157
theologians 21, 42, 215, 244
Theologica Germanica 32
theology 20, 22–3, 77, 142, 154,
177, 179, 195, 210, 219, 227,
237
therapeutic community 209–12
therapeutic prison 224
therapy 139, 157, 183, 186, 209–12,
224
Thessalonians 29
Thomas, R.S. 20, 213–14
thoughts of suicide 144–5, 149, 186
time 85–7
Timothy 189, 249
Tirmidhi 50
torture 172
total institutions 182
Toynbee, Polly 20
training 139, 150, 157, 160, 244
Training Prisons 209
trauma 110, 142, 171
treatment 139, 156–7, 159
Trevor, William 88
trials 71, 81, 86, 91, 110, 138, 279
Trinitarians 96, 216
Trinity 130–1, 277
trust 129, 135, 137, 192, 200
Tudors 259
Turks 253

Uganda 58
unconscious 180
unemployment 108, 191
uniforms 182, 195, 198, 230
United Nations (UN) 44, 57
United States (US) 54, 56, 58, 220
United Synagogue Visitation
Committee 53
useless presence 135

The prison world is one that is largely hidden from our view, secret and removed. Part of the reason for this secrecy may be a fear that we will discover something of ourselves in those in prison. In *Inside Faith*, William Noblett attempts to bring the secrecy to light through the stories of individuals, and to bring to view something of the ministry of chaplains, and others, in a complex, emotional and sometimes violent environment.

Taking the form of short reflections, William Noblett explores real situations that arise in prison life and offers theological insights, along with prayers and narratives that can be used in a prison, liturgical, or house-group setting.

Inside Faith is an invaluable resource book for anyone wishing to know more about prisons, and prison ministry, as well as all those involved in more formal chaplaincy work.

WILLIAM NOBLETT is Chaplain General and Archdeacon of HM Prisons and Chaplain to The Queen.

Cover image by Chad Baker/Stone/gettyimages; design by Judy Linard.

ISBN 978-0-232-52733-9

DARTON · LONGMAN

£14.95.

www.dltbooks.com